A TABLE
IN THE
WILDERNESS

---

*Daily meditations from
the ministry of*

WATCHMAN NEE

VICTORY PRESS
LONDON & EASTBOURNE

© Angus I. Kinnear 1965
Paperback edition 1969

ISBNs

Hardback 85476 081 4
Paperback 85476 165 9

Reprinted 1970
Reprinted 1971
Reprinted 1972 (twice)
Reprinted 1973 (twice)
Reprinted 1974
Reprinted 1975 (twice)
Reprinted 1976

Printed in Great Britain for
VICTORY PRESS (Evangelical Publishers Ltd.),
Lottbridge Drove, Eastbourne, Sussex,
by Richard Clay (The Chaucer Press), Ltd.,
Bungay, Suffolk

PREFACE

"I, JOHN, your brother and partaker with you in the tribulation and kingdom and patience which are in Jesus, was in the isle that is called Patmos, for the word of God and the testimony of Jesus. I was in the Spirit on the Lord's day, and I heard behind me a great voice, as of a trumpet saying, What thou seest write in a book." We sometimes wish God would speak thus again, perhaps through a servant of His incarcerated in some twentieth-century prison cell, to grant us, in this day of heightened spiritual conflict, some new flash of divine light upon our road ahead.

Along with many other faithful servants of Jesus Christ in modern China, Nee To-sheng, or Watchman Nee as he likes to be called, is in fact so situated. But from such as he no recent writings are of course available, and this book contains none. It is derived once again from his earlier ministry of the Word in days when God was using him widely in that land for the salvation of souls and the building and spread of His Church and Kingdom.

Yet we have no reason to believe that the author's thoughts on this theme are any different now from the day when he wrote: "John's first vision was not of events but of Jesus Christ Himself. A knowledge of coming events will only stimulate our curiosity. Even John the beloved disciple must first have a sight of his eternal Lord that shattered him to the dust. Only such a sight creates warriors. Not till we see Him thus are we equipped for conflict. For Christ is the answer to all our questions. Get clear first about Him, and we shall know all we need to know about 'things to come'. He is the risen and victorious King of kings. All the ensuing events are the outcome of His being that."

Let us follow this lead as, day by day, we share the author's meditations on the glories of Christ. If by them we can be fortified to meet the challenge of our times, then the human history which lies behind this book will not have been in vain.

In addition to much fresh material from private sources, this collection includes some extracts from earlier published books and booklets.

Unless otherwise indicated, Scripture quotations are from the English Revised Version of 1885.

ANGUS I. KINNEAR

JANUARY 1st

Looking up to heaven, he blessed and brake the loaves; and he gave to the disciples to set before them. Mark 6. 41.

Surely the one fundamental need in our life and service for God is the blessing of God upon it. No other need exists. What do we mean by blessing? Blessing is the working of God where there is nothing to account for His working. For instance, you calculate that a penny should buy a pennyworth. But if you have not paid your penny, and God has given you ten thousand pennyworth, then you have no basis for your calculations. When five loaves provide food for five thousand and leave twelve baskets of fragments—when, that is to say, the fruit of our service is out of all proportion to the gifts we possess, that is blessing. Or, to be rather extreme, when, taking account of our failures and weaknesses, there should be no fruit at all from our labours, and still there is fruit—that is blessing. Blessing is fruit out of all relation to what we are, results that are not just the working of cause and effect. Blessing comes when God works wholly beyond our reckoning, for His Name's sake.

JANUARY 2nd

O LORD, our Lord, How excellent is thy name in all the earth! Psalm 8. 1 and 9.

In an hour when men are blaspheming the Lord's name, the psalmist can only exclaim in wonder at its greatness. Though himself a poet, he is at a loss for words to express its worth. All he can do is cry "How excellent!" And this unspeakable excellence is "in all the earth". Here, surely is an echo of Genesis 1, where all God beheld "was very good". But having begun thus, the writer concludes his psalm with an identical tribute to the excellent Name, and this without so much as a mention of the Fall of man. Had *we* been writing, we would have felt bound to bring that in. But God is unchanging, and to the psalmist even Adam's sin could not reverse His intention that in the end *man* should "have dominion". For at this point the Lord Jesus steps in. It is Hebrews 2 that illumines Psalm 8. He is that Man, and He has already dealt with sin. In Him all God's desire is realized, and *He is related to us*. There is no deviation in the ways of God: they go straight forward. "O Lord, how excellent!"

JANUARY 3rd

Buying up the opportunity, because the days are evil.
Ephesians 5. 16 mg.

In God's appointed course for you, it may be that today was to have been the greatest day of your life; yet you would let it slip as if it were any other day. The man whose today is like his yesterday lacks a sense of God's timings. No servant of the Lord should be content with present attainment; for to be satisfied with what is, is to be a loser of opportunities.

Let us suppose that on January 3rd the Lord puts it into my heart to go and seek out a certain person who, in His providence, is destined to become five years hence a mighty instrument in His hands for the salvation of souls. To obey may be the greatest single act of service in my life. But suppose on this day I am afraid of the cold, or something equally trivial, and do not go. I have let slip an opportunity, and perhaps lost thereby a powerful instrument for God. And the trouble is, such occasions do not wait for us. They pass swiftly by. So when God moves, let us move with Him. No divinely sent opportunity must elude us.

JANUARY 4th

Working together with him we intreat also that ye receive not the grace of God in vain. 2 Corinthians 6. 1.

God has saved us for Himself. "I press on," says Paul, "if so be that I may apprehend that for which also I was apprehended of Christ Jesus." We were not apprehended for eternal salvation only, but for a quite definite purpose now: to be God's fellow-workers. What is His work today? It is to sum up all things in Christ; to leave no odds and ends of any kind in the universe out of harmony with His exalted Son. How can I cooperate with God? How can I even touch so great a work? I do not know; but with Paul, I want above all things to apprehend that.

JANUARY 5th

By the grace of God I am what I am. 1 Corinthians 15. 10.

Has the manner of God's working in relation to your own life come home to you? Have you not been arrested by the way in which He has moved, choosing you out from multitudes around you and making you His own? Oh, I think of it often. When I was saved I was a student. I had over four hundred fellow students, and out of all that number God's choice lighted on me. How could it have come about? I was one of a large clan, and out of the whole clan God chose me. How could it happen? When we think of the marvellous ways by which His grace reached us we fall down before Him in adoration and acknowledge that He is God, He alone.

You ask why He saved you? Let me tell you that He saved you because it was His delight to save you. Because He wanted you, He chose you and brought you to Himself. So there is nothing for you to say, nothing for you to do, nothing but just to worship Him.

JANUARY 6th

Thou preparest a table before me in the presence of mine enemies: thou hast anointed my head with oil; my cup runneth over. Psalm 23. 5.

Our brother Paul made a great and noble statement to the Philippians. To these who, in material things, were almost his sole supporters he dared to say: "I have all things and abound." Paul gave no hint of need, but took the position of a wealthy child of a wealthy Father, and he had no fears that by so doing he might discourage further supplies. It may be quite in order for an apostle to say to an unbeliever who is himself in distress: "Silver and gold have I none." It would never do for him to say the same thing to believers ready and eager to respond to any appeal for help. It dishonours the Lord when a representative of His discloses needs that would provoke pity on the part of his hearers. If we have a living faith in God, we shall always make our boast in Him.

JANUARY 7th

If, while we were enemies, we were reconciled to God through the death of his Son, much more, being reconciled, shall we be saved by his life. Romans 5. 10.

God makes it quite clear in His Word that to every human need He has but one answer: His Son Jesus Christ. In all His dealings with us He works by taking *us* out of the way and substituting Christ in our place. The Son of God died instead of us for our forgiveness; He lives instead of us for our deliverance. So we can speak of two substitutions: a Substitute on the Cross who secures our forgiveness and a Substitute within who secures our victory. It will help us greatly, and save us from much confusion, if we keep constantly before us this fact, that God will answer all our questions in one way only, namely, by showing us more of His Son.

JANUARY 8th

There is the sound of abundance of rain. 1 Kings 18. 41.

How utterly Elijah ventured everything on his God! For three and a half years there had been a nation-wide drought, and water was very scarce indeed. Yet he insisted it be poured lavishly on the sacrifice that was to vindicate Jehovah. "What! squander our precious reserves of water, with no rain in sight?" "Pour it on," said Elijah. "Do it a second time; do it a third!" And not content with that, he himself took a hand in filling the surrounding trench with water.

If we too are to see God vindicated, we must bring what we have and let it go to Him. "But what will happen if rain doesn't come?" you protest. "I must hold on to the water I have." God forbid! That way lies drought and barrenness. Let it go to Him! What you lose will be nothing when compared to His abundance of rain.

JANUARY 9th

Let the saints exult in glory; let them sing for joy upon their beds. Psalm 149. 5.

Here is a picture of Christians who are truly in the enjoyment of Christ's victory. They repose triumphant on their beds, joyously at rest in Him. Consider what this position signifies. Their backs are to the earth, setting the world behind them as it were, while their faces are up to heaven, keeping eternal values always in their view. Such "beds" as theirs are no mere couches of ease, but platforms of effective service. Are you perhaps forced to lie in bed? May the high praises of God still be in your mouth!

JANUARY 10th

Why do the nations rage? Psalm 2. 1.

The answer is supplied at once. It is because "the rulers take counsel together against the Lord, and against his anointed". However violent the hostility between them, world governments are at heart united on one thing: they are against the reign of Christ. We look upon the nations as some of them bad, some good; but Scripture points us to the "prince of this world" behind them all. Prompted by him, earth's rulers today seek only absolute freedom from the sanctions imposed by the law of Christ. They want no more love, no more humility, no more truth. "Let us break their bands asunder," they cry, "and cast away their cords from us."

At this point alone in all Scripture is God said to laugh. His King is already on His holy hill! The early Church was very much aware of Christ's dominion. More than ever today do we need to remember it. Soon, maybe in our lifetime, He will shepherd the nations with a rod of iron. Our task is to plead with men to "be wise"; to "put their trust in Him".

JANUARY 11th

Yet I will rejoice in the Lord, I will joy in the God of my salvation. Habakkuk 3. 18.

When the Galilean boy brought his bread to Jesus, what did Jesus do with it? He broke it. God will always break what is offered to Him. He breaks what He takes, then blesses and uses it to meet men's needs. Is not this true to your experience and mine? You give yourself to the Lord, and at once everything goes so badly wrong that you are tempted to find fault with His ways. To persist in such an attitude is to be broken, yes indeed, but to what purpose? You have gone too far for the world to use you, but you have not gone far enough for God. This is the tragedy of many a Christian. Do we want Him to use us? Then day by day let us go on giving to Him, not finding fault with His methods, but accepting His handling of us with praise and expectation.

JANUARY 12th

These were purchased from among men, to be the first fruits unto God and unto the Lamb. Revelation 14. 4.

My home province of Fukien is famous for its oranges. I would say (though doubtless I am prejudiced) that there are none like them anywhere in the world. As you look out on the hills at the beginning of the orange season, all the groves are green. But if you observe more carefully you will see, scattered here and there on the trees, golden oranges already showing up. It is a beautiful sight to see the flecks of gold dotted among the dark green trees. Later the whole crop will ripen and the groves will turn to gold, but now it is these firstfruits that are gathered. They are carefully hand-picked, and it is they that fetch the top market-prices, often as much as three times the price of the harvest.

All Christians will reach ripeness somehow, we are assured. But the Lamb seeks firstfruits for His hour of supreme demand.

JANUARY 13th

Abram said unto Lot, Let there be no strife, I pray thee, between me and thee, and between my herdmen and thy herdmen; for we are brethren. Is not the whole land before thee? Genesis 13. 8f.

To Abram, newly returned from his misguided venture to Egypt, how precious must have seemed the land which God had given him! Now however he was to learn an important new lesson, namely, not to grasp at its possession. "But surely," he might have reasoned, "so precious a gift ought to be seized and held fast at all costs!" And so do we reason when God gives us His gifts. But Abram saw that he must relinquish his grip. His nephew Lot should be given first choice of all he wanted.

This is a lesson we must all learn. Can we trust God to keep for us what He has given, never laying hold on it ourselves in our natural desire for possession? What God gives, he *gives*! We need not struggle to retain it. Indeed if we grasp it fearfully and hold on, we may risk losing it. Only what we have let go in committal to Him becomes in fact really ours.

JANUARY 14th

Joseph is a fruitful bough, a fruitful bough by a fountain; his branches run over the wall. The archers have sorely grieved him, and shot at him, and persecuted him: but his bow abode in strength. Genesis 49. 22 f.

Of the many typical servants of God in the Old Testament, Joseph is perhaps the most perfect. Yet while Scripture reveals no apparent flaw in his character, we know well that his was no easy pathway. When did his troubles begin? Surely with his dreams. They represent spiritual vision. In them he saw what God would do, and his own place in the divine plan. It was his dreams that started things off, for he saw what his brothers could not see. "This dreamer," they called him, and plotted his downfall. So he was sold for a servant and lay in chains of iron (Psalm 105. 17 f.). Yet Joseph could survive it all to become at length God's means of fulfilling a mighty purpose for His people. He stands firm to the end who can *see*.

JANUARY 15th

*Jehovah-jireh: as it is said to this day, In the mount of the
Lord it shall be provided.* Genesis 22. 14.

The only question Isaac is ever said to have asked of
his own accord was "Where is the lamb for a burnt offering?"
The answer was categorical: "God will provide." This is
typical of Isaac, whose privilege as heir was simply to receive
what was freely bestowed by his father. He did not have to dig
wells; the most required of him was to re-open those his father
had dug. Nor indeed had he any say in his own marriage; he
was not consulted about the woman, and was not expected to
make any efforts to seek her out. Even the tomb in which he
was buried had already been purchased by his father.

We too, like Isaac, have been born into a wealthy home.
What God our Father has provided for us, we are expected to
receive. The God of Isaac is our God, and is He not God the
Giver?

JANUARY 16th

*Whosoever shall call on the name of the Lord shall be
saved.* Acts 2. 21.

How is this possible? Because God has fulfilled that
other prophecy of Joel, that "I will pour forth my Spirit upon
all flesh". Because the Holy Spirit has been poured out upon
all mankind, the merest cry from the sinner to God is enough.

No preacher of the Gospel is of much use unless he believes
this. The Holy Spirit's proximity to the sinner is vital to our
preaching. God in the heavens is too far beyond man's reach.

But "Say not in thy heart, who shall ascend into heaven? that is, to bring Christ down: . . . The word is nigh thee." I always believe the Holy Spirit is upon a man when I preach Christ to him, just as He was upon the waters at the creation. He is waiting to bring Christ into his life. His ministry is like the daylight. Open the window-shutters even a little, and it floods in and illumines the whole interior. Let there be but a cry from the heart to God, and in that instant the Spirit enters and begins His transforming work of conviction, repentance and faith—the miracle of new birth.

JANUARY 17th

Repent ye, and be baptized every one of you in the name of Jesus Christ unto the remission of your sins: and ye shall receive the gift of the Holy Ghost. Acts 2. 38.

Suppose I went into a book-shop, selected a two-volume book, and having put down the price, walked out of the shop carelessly leaving one volume on the counter. When I discovered the oversight, what should I do? I should go straight back to recover the forgotten volume, but I should not dream of paying anything for it. I should simply remind the shopkeeper that both volumes were duly paid for, thank him again for the second one, and without further ado march happily out of the shop with my possession under my arm. Would you not do the same under the same circumstances?

But you *are* under the same circumstances. If you have fulfilled the conditions you are entitled to two gifts, not just one. You have already taken the remission of your sins. Why not just come, and if you have never done so, thank Him for the gift of the Holy Ghost *now*?

JANUARY 18th

It was the good pleasure of God . . . to reveal his Son in me. Galatians 1. 15 f.

I would not, if I could, exchange places with the disciples, even on the Mount of Transfiguration. The Christ with whom they lived was a Christ limited by time and space. Was He in Galilee? Then He could not be found in Jerusalem. Was He in Jerusalem? Then men sought Him in vain in Galilee. But today Christ is limited neither by time nor space, for He lives in the power of an endless life, and the Father has been pleased to reveal Him in my heart. He was with them sometimes; He is with me always. They knew Him then after the flesh, saw Him, touched Him, lived with Him in the closest contact. "Now know we him so no more", and yet I know Him in truth, for I know Him as God is pleased He should be known. Has He not given me the spirit of wisdom and revelation in the knowledge of Him?

JANUARY 19th

Wherefore, O King Agrippa, I was not disobedient unto the heavenly vision. Acts 26. 19.

What called forth Paul's lifelong consecration of himself was that flash of light from heaven. The obedience sprang from the vision. For while it remains true that all self-committal to God is precious to Him, blind self-committal may not serve Him very far. There is, I think, a difference between the initial, pure but uninstructed consecration that follows our conversion and that further giving of ourselves that may spring out of a seeing of the plan of God. Upon the one, based as it is on *our* salvation, He may not at once make severe demands. But when He opens His heart to reveal to us what *He* wants done, and when having asked for our willingness He receives our fresh response, then it is that His demands upon our giving intensify. We have pledged our word on the basis of a new understanding, and He takes us anew at our word. Hereafter all we have must go into it, all the way.

JANUARY 20th

When the cloud was taken up from over the tabernacle, the children of Israel went onward. Exodus 40. 36.

Just as all God's speaking to His people in those far-off days was from between the cherubim of glory, so all His leading of them onward was by means of that same glory. In the cloud by day and the fire by night the glory of God appeared, and by it they moved. For us, too, all revelation of God's will issues from His glory. See the glory of God in relation to any matter and we have discovered God's leading in regard to it. You ask me "Is this His will? Is that?" I reply by asking in turn, "Is God's glory resting there?" Discern that, and you need wait for nothing further. For the divine glory itself expresses the divine will. Guidance is thus simply a matter of correspondence to that. Where God's glory rests we need not ask the way.

JANUARY 21st

Go not up, for the Lord is not among you; that ye be not smitten down before your enemies. Numbers 14. 42.

There is always the serious possibility that God will change His mind. This fact should keep us in humble fear before Him. For if there is something in us which resists His will, God may be compelled to modify His orders to us, as He did to Israel. It is true they acknowledged they had sinned, but they were wrong in thinking they could then proceed as though nothing had altered. It had. In such a situation it is folly to hold blindly on to something the Lord gave us twenty years ago—or even last year. We must live in today, and hold on *to God*. It is the present relationship that is vital. Why, even Moses found his course redirected when he failed God. But bowing to God's present will he was blessed, whereas the Israelites who tried to ignore it met only disaster. Has something in me altered God's mind? Let me then be open to His adjustment. One day He will restore.

JANUARY 22nd

Alas, my master! how shall we do? 2 Kings 6. 15.

When God works His miracle, we have to laugh at our own foolishness. If we still persist in worrying and planning, then we are no disciples of His. Many, I fear, never see God work for them because they always have a way out— some friend perhaps, who might help a little if God does not! Most to be pitied are those who, brought to a supreme crisis, still find an avenue of escape. For necessity is the foundation for miracles. To escape the one is to miss the other. Great difficulties are meant only to force us out of ourselves into reliance on Him. When there is no way forward or back, then God is able. He has a plan. So do not fear impossibilities. They are of no account to Him. Fall at His feet and wait for Him to act. A miracle is ahead.

JANUARY 23rd

Martha, Martha, thou art anxious and troubled about many things: but one thing is needful. Luke 10. 41f.

Let us be frank: work for the Lord has its attractions. It can thrill you when crowds gather to hear you preach. If instead you are compelled to stay at home, occupied from morning to night with mundane affairs, you soon begin to think: "How meaningless life is! How grand to get out and serve the Lord! If only I were free to go round preaching!"

But that is not spirituality. It may be no more than a yielding to natural preference. Is it not possible that much of our so-called service for Him is simply the pursuit of our own inclinations? We are so restless we cannot bear to stay at home, so we run around doing God's work for our own relief. We may be doing our utmost to serve our brethren, and we may be labouring to save sinners, but one thing is needful. Are we first of all ministering to Him?

JANUARY 24th

The Lord God hath given me the tongue of them that are taught, that I should know how to speak a word in season to him that is weary. Isaiah 50. 4 mg.

Am I afraid to speak without the consciousness that what I utter has come to me here and now from God? Must I be so painfully concerned as to whether or not it is the Spirit who is moving me to say this or that? In demanding to be so conscious that what I say is indeed from God, may I merely be displaying how spiritually poor I am? A wealthy Christian speaks out of the abundance of grace in his life. Waking morning by morning to be taught in God's Word, he amasses spiritual riches on which to draw. Instead of ekeing out a hand-to-mouth existence on special dispensations of grace, he is laying up over the years a permanent overplus, out of which to bring forth things new and old. From such experience he can, if need be, speak the mind of the Spirit without the overweening consciousness of being God's immediate oracle.

JANUARY 25th

Our God whom we serve is able to deliver us from the burning fiery furnace. Daniel 3. 17.

How does the Church reach her goal? Only by travelling the pathway from pressure to enlargement, from poverty to enrichment. You ask: What do we mean by enlargement through pressure? When three are shut into a furnace and the three become four, that is enlargement through pressure. Some find a furnace rather close quarters for three, so they seek a way of escape; others accept the limitation, and in accepting it, make room for a Fourth. Not to let difficulties shut us out from God, but to let them shut us in to Him, that is enlargement through pressure. Some, through pressure, reach God's end; others come to an end in the pressure. Some die in straitness; others, through straitness, find fulness of life. Some murmur when trials befall, finding in them only restraint, limitation and death; others praise God for the trials, and in doing so discover the pathway to enlargement, liberation and abundance of life.

JANUARY 26th

When Jesus therefore had received the vinegar, he said, It is finished. John 19. 30.

The Christian Faith begins not with a big DO but with a big DONE. Of course our reason protests at this. If we do not get moving, how can we ever reach the goal? What can we attain without effort? How can we ever achieve anything if we do not work for it? But Christianity is a queer business! It begins from rest. If at the outset we try to do anything, we get nothing; if we seek to attain, we miss it all. "It is finished," said Jesus, and Paul opens his letter to the Ephesians with the statement that God *has* blessed us with every spiritual blessing in the heavenly places in Christ. We are invited at the very outset therefore to rest and enjoy what God has done; not to try to attain it for ourselves.

JANUARY 27th

Behold I make a covenant: before all thy people I will do marvels. Exodus 34. 10.

Many of us do not differentiate clearly between the promises of God, the accomplished facts of God (His mighty works), and the covenant of God. Promises are given to encourage faith, but often we cannot rise to God's promises. At times we cannot even lay hold of divine facts; appearances seem to belie them. But when this is so we still have His covenant. And the covenant means more than the promises, more even than the mighty works. It is something God has committed Himself to do. The covenant is a handle given us by God on which faith can lay hold. Morally we have no claim on God. But He has been pleased to bind Himself to a covenant, and having thus pledged Himself to act for us, He is— and I say it reverently—bound to do so. Herein is the preciousness of the covenant. It is this that gives strength to faith when faith is at its weakest.

JANUARY 28th

Whom the Lord loveth he chasteneth, and scourgeth every son whom he receiveth. Hebrews 12. 6.

It seems clear that spiritual vision by itself is not enough to transform a life. Consider Jacob's ladder. Because of his crooked behaviour, Jacob had lost home and possessions. Yet in spite of this God favoured him at Bethel with a vision so marvellous that he was moved to exclaim, "How dreadful is this place!" The promises that accompanied it were full and unconditional. Yet contrast with them the words of his response to God: "If . . . if . . . if . . . then I will. . . ." Even with God he wanted to do a business deal. He was the same unchanged Jacob.

Soon, however, he was to become involved with Laban, who was just such another as himself. By this and other means, God took Jacob through years of the most fruitful discipline. The spoilt son of the house became a harshly treated labourer. But His ways are always right, and it was a new Jacob who found his way back to Bethel in the end.

JANUARY 29th

I will be as the dew unto Israel. Hosea 14. 5.

These words describe the beginning of everything in the experience of God's children. Dewfall is altogether vital to the life and growth of trees and flowers; and to us the Lord Himself promises to be as the dew. Everything in our life as Christians comes down to us from Christ as source. He is made unto us wisdom, righteousness, holiness—yes, everything, and there is no human need that we shall find unmet as we receive Him, nor indeed will anything be given to us as a separate gift apart from Him.

"I will be as the dew," He affirms, and in the next half of the verse Hosea shows how life with this as its foundation takes on a mysterious dual character. In it the blossom of the lily is wonderfully linked with the roots of the cedar: frail beauty and massive strength united in a single plant. Such miracles are wrought by heaven's dewfall alone.

JANUARY 30th

He shall blossom as the lily, and cast forth his roots as Lebanon. Hosea 14. 5.

Here united in the child of God are two contrasting characters. Above ground, as it were, is the simple unsophisticated life of trust and faith represented by the lily of God's planting. That is what men see. Yet buried deep down out of sight, giving to this frail plant a wholly unsuspected strength, are the massive roots of the cedar. Here surely is the paradox of a life in which the Cross is known. Outwardly it is fragile as the lily blooming on the earth, but secretly there is a hundred times more below ground.

This is the test. How much of my life is seen? When men look on the surface, have they seen the whole, or is there something more? Have I in the unseen a secret history with God? Men take account only of the lily blooming in its weakness. God is concerned with the roots, that they shall be cedar-like in strength.

JANUARY 31st

I am as strong this day as in the day that Moses sent me; as my strength was then, even so is my strength now, for war and to go out and to come in. Joshua 14. 11.

It is a distressing fact that some of us who have proved God's saving power yet doubt His power to keep. Do we not realize that He who is the Giver of grace is the One also who maintains us in His grace? Look at Caleb. Strong as he had been in the day Moses sent him to spy out the land, he was no less strong now as he uttered these words. Moreover what had proved sufficient for the ordinary demands of daily life was equal too to the special stresses of war. Hard years had intervened; yet his vigour at eighty-five was no less than at forty. There is but one explanation of his experience, as indeed there will be of ours at the end. He had been kept by the power of God.

FEBRUARY 1st

Rejoice alway; . . . in everything give thanks. 1 Thessalonians 5. 16.

How is this possible? How can we rejoice amid difficulties? Where does that joy come from? We cannot manufacture it, for if we have not got it we just have not got it! But elsewhere Paul gives us the secret. We are to rejoice in the Lord. We are to live by the joy of Him who, where you or I would have despaired, "rejoiced in spirit" with those triumphant words: "Father . . . it was well-pleasing in thy sight!" (Luke 10. 21). His joy is yours. Learn to live by it above your troubles. When tempted to be cast down, look up and ask yourself, Has the Lord lost His joy today? Only if He has may you be content to be joyless! For it is not a question of your joy, but His. The joy of the Lord is your strength.

FEBRUARY 2nd

Oh that thou wouldest bless me indeed, . . . and that thou wouldest keep me from evil, that it be not to my sorrow.
1 Chronicles 4. 10.

A life of blessing should be the normal life of a Christian. His one concern must be in no way to obstruct that blessing's flow. If it is withheld there is a cause, and the explanation is not to be sought in outward things. On one occasion I observed a Christian worker at variance with another. I listened to him protesting that he had been right, and indeed there was nothing wrong with what he said nor with the thing he had done. But I thought to myself: Brother, you may be perfectly correct, but if our rightness lacks the blessing of the Lord, what does it profit?

In the work of God, all has failed when the blessing of God has failed. If we are set on knowing God's favour, we shall find limitations imposed on the words we utter, and on our whole manner of life. For rightness is not our goal. The test of our actions is not, Are they right or wrong? but always and only, Is the divine blessing upon them?

FEBRUARY 3rd

Was not Esau Jacob's brother? saith the Lord; yet I loved Jacob. Malachi 1. 2.

God has indeed said "Jacob I loved, but Esau I hated" (Romans 9. 13), and whom He loves He blesses. This is a very solemn matter. David failed and Abraham made mistakes, Isaac was weak and Jacob crafty, yet the blessing of God was with them all. You, today, may be a much better fellow than Jacob, but without the divine favour where are you? Learn to set high store by the blessing of God, and to view with suspicion anything that would cause you to forfeit it. Maybe you have been tempted to despise some brother less endowed with gifts than you, and yet God blesses him! And you? Again and again you have done the right thing, and yet His blessing has been withheld. Dare you say God has erred? Beware of taking offence at His choices. Envy of another man's calling can work havoc in our own. Our fruitfulness for God depends upon His blessing, but it is all too possible by our speech, our attitude, our opinions, to arrest its flow. Let us trust God so to deal with us that, without His blessing, we cannot live!

FEBRUARY 4th

The things that are despised, did God choose, yea and the things that are not. 1 Corinthians 1. 28.

The Cross is the greatest leveller in the universe. It brings every one of us to zero. It offers the whole of mankind a new beginning. The difference between a Christian who progresses fast and one who progresses slowly is in the faithfulness and obedience of the former, never in anything he possesses by nature. There are many things too strong and too imposing for God to use. Instead He not only chooses the weak things and the despised: He goes further. The apostle seems almost at a loss to know how to define the things, so weak and despicable in men's eyes, that God elects to use. In a telling phrase he sums them up as the "things which are not".

Do *you* fall in that category? Do not despair. Far from being at a disadvantage as compared with others, you may in fact have the edge over them. For at least you are already at zero, and have not a long way still to go to reach God's starting point! Simply believe Him, and obey.

FEBRUARY 5th

Abraham prayed unto God: and God healed Abimelech, and his wife, and his maidservants; and they bare children. Genesis 20. 17.

It is striking evidence of the spiritual life of this man of God that he could pray for children to be granted to others while his prayers for his own wife were still unanswered. He interceded for Abimelech, and God heard.

It is difficult to understand Abraham's reversion to that half-lie about Sarah being his sister, especially in view of the deep fellowship with God which had just preceded it. But this time he discloses that the arrangement made between them dated right back to Mesopotamia. Some hidden root of unbelief and fear had lingered through all these years, and now at length had come to light. At the start of his wanderings Abraham seems to have feared Sarah might be separated from him. Yet surely by now he should have known God would take full responsibility to see this did not happen.

At last, here in Gerar, the lurking fear was dragged out into the light of day, and slain, leaving Abraham free to pray for others. He did not pray for Sarah. Now he had no need to. Immediately after this Isaac was born.

FEBRUARY 6th

When therefore he said unto them, I am he, they went backward, and fell to the ground. John 18. 6.

On that last night before Calvary, everything seemed to be going wrong. Betrayal and denial were in the air; people were hiding, or running away naked in their eagerness to escape. But to those who had come to take Him Jesus said so peacefully and quietly, "I am he." It was they who were nervous and who fell backward. This inward peace always marked Him. He could sleep through the storm. He could register the touch of faith amidst the jostlings of an impatient crowd, and ask who it was had touched Him. "My peace", He terms it.

This peace, He said, "I leave with you." He did not take it away, for He is here. So the martyrs of old displayed it too. They might be tortured or burnt, but they had about them a quiet dignity none could gainsay. Yes, in the world we shall have our troubles, but we shall have also His peace, which, the apostle Paul affirms, is beyond understanding.

FEBRUARY 7th

Peace I leave with you; my peace I give unto you. John 14. 27.

It is not just a question of peace but of "My peace". It is not only that God gives me peace but that "the peace of God", the deep undisturbedness of God, keeps my heart (Philippians 4. 7). We get troubled when things go wrong, but let us realize something else. God chose this world to be the arena of His plan, the centre of what He has set Himself to do. He had a definite purpose, which Satan came in and interfered with, and yet in spite of that (the implications of which we realize very little) He maintains a deep untroubled peace. He is not afraid to wait another thousand years if need be. *That* is the peace which is given to us.

Paul says the peace of God should be a garrison for my

heart. What does that mean? It means that a foe must first fight through the garrison to reach me. The garrison must be overcome before my heart can be touched. So I dare to be as peaceful as God, for the peace of God—that peace which is keeping God—is keeping me.

FEBRUARY 8th

Christ having come a high priest of the good things to come, . . . through his own blood, entered in once for all into the holy place, having obtained eternal redemption.
Hebrews 9. 11 f.

If I would appreciate the value of the Blood of Christ, I must accept God's valuation of it, for the Blood is not primarily for me, but for God. Nothing illustrates this fact so clearly as the account of the Day of Atonement. In Leviticus 16 we read how on that day the blood was taken from the sin offering and brought into the Most Holy Place, and there sprinkled before the Lord seven times. The offering of course was public, in the court of the tabernacle and in full view of the people. But into the Sanctuary itself no man entered save the high priest. Alone he sprinkled the atoning blood there before God, away from the eyes of the men who were to benefit by it. We must be very clear about this. The precious Blood of Christ is in the first place for *God*, not man, to see. A holy and righteous God has accepted it and professed Himself satisfied, and our valuation of it stems from this profound fact.

FEBRUARY 9th

Grace and truth came by Jesus Christ. John 1. 17.

This statement is the key to all that follows in John's Gospel. Right through it you find the same double emphasis, upon truth on the one hand and upon grace on the other. Truth will always make demands, and grace will always be there to meet them. In the incident recorded in Chapter 8 of the woman taken in adultery, truth shines forth. The Lord did not say to her "It is all right; you have not sinned." He did not suggest to the Jews that what she had done was nothing serious, and that He was not deeply concerned about it. No, His words were: "He that is without sin among you, let him first cast a stone at her." The truth was there: she had indeed sinned, and according to the law she should be stoned; but so also was the grace, for when all had departed He turned to her with "Neither do I condemn thee". Throughout the Gospel of John you will find truth is always matched by grace in this way.

FEBRUARY 10th

When Abram was ninety years old and nine, the Lord appeared to Abram, and said unto him, I am God Almighty; walk before me, and be thou perfect. Genesis 17.1.

God did not say this to the strong Abram, he who in Ishmael could produce a son. He waited until His servant was quite incapable, even had he wanted to, of repeating the action. Then, and then only, God came to him with this new unveiling of Himself as God Almighty.

There is no sign that Abram had repented of his action. Rather does it appear that Ishmael was becoming more precious to him. Had he then not realized his error? Had he not sought after God? If indeed he had not, we might say that from a human standpoint there was not much hope for him. Hope, however, depended not so much on whether *he* wanted God but on whether *God* wanted him. And God certainly did! He was still at work in His servant. He had not let him go. "Learn that I am all-powerful," God said, "and then walk in the light of that knowledge." For "be perfect" means, among other things, "be perfect in weakness," letting God Almighty do it all.

FEBRUARY 11th

Unto him that sitteth on the throne, and unto the Lamb, be the blessing and the honour and the glory and the dominion, for ever and ever. Revelation 5. 13.

To worship the creature rather than the Creator is an inbred tendency with us. In this even John himself had to be pulled up. For all the conflict depicted in this book of Revelation turns on this issue. All the war in heaven, all the tribulation on earth, stems alike from Satan's attempt to steal to himself God's praise. But here in Revelation 5 on this great coronation day, all in heaven and earth and beneath the earth and on the sea unite to acclaim Christ as supreme. The chapter closely matches Philippians 2 with its "every knee should bow . . . every tongue should confess that Jesus Christ is Lord". The death of the cross has brought this outcome; it is the newly slain Lamb who is worthy.

FEBRUARY 12th

Concerning the work of my hands, command ye me.
Isaiah 45. 11.

Here in Time, God is not free. He does not move His children about like pawns on a board, but has limited Himself to their free choice. Wittingly He has done this, knowing what it will bring Him in the end. In eternity past God was unlimited; there was no second will. Again in eternity future He will be unlimited, for love will have conquered and man's free-will will be one with His. That is His glory.

But now, in Time, God has limited Himself. Only as men of freewill are with Him today can He accomplish His purpose. And freewill means I can obey or not, as I choose. It is as though God had put at our disposal a locomotive of immense power, and we were told to lay the track. The power is there, and the destination is planned, but the engine does not control the rails. It is the rails that have power to limit the engine. "Ask whatsoever ye will, and it shall be done unto you." How great is our responsibility!

FEBRUARY 13th

What things soever ye shall bind on earth shall be bound in heaven: and what things soever ye shall loose on earth shall be loosed in heaven. Matthew 18. 18.

"What things soever": these are precious words. Here heaven is measured by earth, for there is always more power in heaven than the measure of our asking; there is always more to be loosed or bound in heaven than we ask down here. Why do we seek deliverance from sin? Why are we always crying to God for enduement with power? To pray "Thy will be done in me" is a good beginning no doubt, but we must go on to "Thy will be done *on earth*". The children of God today are taken up with far too small things, whereas their prayer is intended for the release of heaven's mighty acts. Prayer for myself or my own immediate concerns must lead on to prayer for the Kingdom. In this the Church should be heaven's outlet, the channel of release for heaven's power, the medium of accomplishment of God's purpose. Many things have accumulated in heaven because God has not yet found His outlet on earth; the Church has not yet prayed.

FEBRUARY 14th

She hath wrought a good work upon me. Matthew 26. 10.

When the Lord returns and we see Him face to face, I trust that we shall all pour out our treasures at His feet. But today—what are we doing today?

Several days after Mary broke the alabaster box and poured the ointment on Jesus' head, there were some women who went early in the morning to anoint His body. Did they do it? Did they succeed in their purpose on that first day of the week? No, He was gone! There was only one soul who in fact succeeded in anointing the body of the Lord, and it was Mary, who anointed Him beforehand. All the others were too late, for He had risen. The pressing question, then, is: What am I doing to the Lord today?

FEBRUARY 15th

Blessed be the God and Father of our Lord Jesus Christ.
1 Peter 1. 3.

This exclamation occurs in the writings of both Peter and Paul, and is one of those things which, by its spontaneity, displays the true spirit of these men. From it we get a glimpse of the man; and God allows this personal element in the message to come through, because it is never merely a question of what we say but of who we are.

It is our privilege to preach the Word, but no single one of us is God's oracle. We cannot utter His words without bringing to them something personal of our own. Many of us can preach a good message, but one spontaneous sentence of ours has the power to confirm or overthrow it all. "Out of the abundance of the heart the mouth speaketh." Humble or defiant, dealt with by the Cross or still whole and unbroken, the truth must come out, for God cannot use play-actors. Our spirit is revealed in our words.

FEBRUARY 16th

The priests that bare the ark of the covenant of the Lord stood firm on dry ground in the midst of Jordan, and all Israel . . . passed clean over Jordan. Joshua 3. 17.

We must have faith to see all God's people brought into their inheritance. That is His purpose, and it will be carried through. But as a means to realizing that purpose, God needs those willing to step right into death if need be, and to stand there steadfast until all are safely over. Because that little band of priests did so, holding firm with the ark in the place where death threatened, a whole nation passed dryshod clean through Jordan. Not one soul remained behind! Of course it was not they, but the ark of God, that opened the way into a land of promise. Never forget that. But note this too: it was they who took it there and held it there. By their act of faith in standing with the Lord amidst death, others passed into abundant life. Am I ready for this?

FEBRUARY 17th

Now he that stablisheth us with you in Christ, and anointed us, is God. 2 Corinthians 1. 21.

The Lord God Himself has put us in Christ. Our destiny is therefore bound up with His. When preaching in the villages of China one must often use very simple illustrations. I remember once I took up a small book, and into it I put a piece of paper. "Now look carefully," I said. "I take this paper. It has an identity of its own, quite separate from this book. Having no other use for it at the moment I put it into the book. Now I do something with the book. I mail it to Shanghai. I do not mail the paper, but the paper has been put into the book. Then where is the paper? Can the book go to Shanghai and the paper remain here? Can the paper have a separate destiny from the book? No, where the book goes the paper goes. If I drop the book in the river the paper goes too, and if I quickly take it out again I recover the paper also. Whatever experience the book goes through the paper goes through with it, for it is still there in the book." To be in Christ is just like that. It is to be identified with Him in all He has gone through. He was crucified. Then must I *ask* God to crucify me? Never! My Saviour's destiny is already become mine.

FEBRUARY 18th

Through love be servants one to another. Galatians 5. 13.

Legalism is bound to produce pride of heart. To live by the law I must exert my strength of will, often against my own inclinations. Such effort inevitably leads me to despise or pity those who are not trying as hard as I, or who are trying and failing. My very exertions give me a superior feeling that sours me towards them, and even though I keep my feeling to myself, I shall soon find I am too aloof even to pray with those I consider less spiritual. Living by the law leads to this. But God is too big to stereotype His saints. People are not to be conformed to me, but to His death. And that is just as well. For sourness in apples is no mark of maturity! Ripe apples are sweet. If God is really producing something in me I shall find no difficulty in going along with other saints whose history is different from mine.

FEBRUARY 19th

Bring forth quickly the best robe and put it on him. Luke 15. 22.

God is so wealthy that His chief delight is to give. His treasure-stores are so full that it is pain to Him when we refuse Him an opportunity of lavishing those treasures upon us. When the prodigal returned home the father had no word of rebuke for the waste nor of inquiry regarding the substance. He only rejoiced over the opportunity his son's return afforded him for spending more. It was the father's joy that he could find in him an applicant for the robe, the ring, the shoes and the feast; it was his sorrow that in the elder son he found no such applicant. It is a grief to the heart of God when we try to provide things for Him. He is so very, very rich. It gives Him true joy when we just let Him give and give and give again to us. He wants to be the Giver eternally, and He wants to be the Doer eternally. If only we saw how rich and how great He is!

FEBRUARY 20th

Hebron became the inheritance of Caleb, because that he wholly followed the Lord. Joshua 14. 14.

"We are well able to overcome" is the declaration of the man or woman whose confidence in the Lord is unqualified. He believes God's promises are trustworthy, and that because He is with His people, victory over every foe is assured. Do you believe this? Many do, but with a faith that vacillates. They sing their song of praise, and the words are right, but there is something hesitant about the tune. With Caleb it was otherwise. He sang the right words firmly, to the right tune. Listen to their brave, ringing tones:

> *"Let us go up at once and possess it;*
> *For we are well able to overcome."*

He had no doubts whatever about his God. But note too the urgency of that first clause: "Let us go up *at once*!" True faith brooks no delay. One who reckons God faithful to His word declares this not merely by doing His will, but by doing it instantly.

We know that the law is spiritual: but I am carnal, sold under sin. Romans 7. 14.

If you have a very clumsy servant and he just sits still and does nothing, then his clumsiness does not appear. If he does nothing all day he will be of little use to you, it is true, but at least he will do no damage that way. But if you say to him: "Now come along, don't idle away your time; get up and do something!" then immediately the trouble begins. He knocks the chair over as he gets up, stumbles over a footstool a few paces further on, then smashes some precious dish as soon as he handles it. If you make no demands upon him his clumsiness is never noticed, but as soon as you ask him to do anything his awkwardness is at once apparent. As with us all, the demands were all right, but the man himself was all wrong! For we are all sinners by nature. The trouble is that without the law we do not know it. So long as God asks nothing of us, all seems to go well. It is when He demands of us something that the occasion is provided for a grand display of our sinfulness, "that through the commandment sin might become exceeding sinful".

I thank God through Jesus Christ our Lord. Romans 7. 25.

"O wretched man that I am! who shall deliver me?" had been Paul's despairing cry. Then in a flash of illumination it changed to this shout of praise.

The first words of the delivered man are most precious: "I

thank God". If someone gives you a cup of water you thank the person who gave it, not someone else. Why did Paul say "Thank God"? Because God was the One who did everything. Had it been Paul who did it, he would have said, "Thank Paul". But he saw that Paul was a "wretched man" and that God alone could meet his need; so he thanked God. God wants to do all, for He must have all the glory. God has done everything on the Cross for our forgiveness and He will do everything in us for our deliverance. In both cases He is the Doer. "It is God that worketh in you. . . ."

FEBRUARY 23rd

And David was afraid of the Lord that day. 2 Samuel 6. 9.

Probably all of us are troubled by this story of the tragic death of Uzzah. David had sinned in ignorance in using a cart to transport the ark of God "which is called by the Name". It seemed a very safe way, but man's ideas, however good, always expose their faultiness. The oxen stumbled, the ark shook, and Uzzah touched it to steady it. He did it warm-heartedly, for the glory of God—and he died instantly. No wonder David was troubled!

The ark protected Israel, not Israel the ark. Who ever heard of a forest-guard protecting tigers? No, God is well able to take care of Himself. Many things which God should do, man does; many times when we should look to Him to speak, we speak; we arrange things which we should wait for God to arrange. "Why shouldn't I preach?" we protest, "I want to." This is the iniquity of our ministry. Has none of us been found out here? But praise God, if we confess our sins, He is faithful and righteous to forgive!

FEBRUARY 24th

When he, the Spirit of truth, is come, he shall guide you into all the truth. John 16. 13.

One thing is certain, that revelation will always precede faith. Seeing and believing are two principles which govern Christian living. When we see something God has done in Christ, our spontaneous rejoinder is faith's "Thank You, Lord!". Revelation is always the work of the Holy Spirit, who by coming alongside and opening to us the Scriptures guides us into all the truth. Count on Him, for He is here for this very thing. And when such difficulties as lack of understanding or lack of faith confront you, always address those difficulties directly to the Lord: "Lord, open my eyes. Make this thing clear to me. Help Thou my unbelief!" He will not let such prayers go unheeded.

FEBRUARY 25th

She opened not the gate for joy, but ran in, and told that Peter stood before the gate. And they said unto her, Thou art mad. Acts 12. 14 f.

Numbers of people have come to me and told of their fears and misgivings even while they have sought to trust the Lord. They have made their requests, they have laid hold of the promises of God, and yet doubts continually arise unbidden. I love to recall that when Peter came back from prison and knocked at the door where the church was at prayer, the believers exclaimed, "It is his angel."

There are people today who claim to have greater faith than those gathered in Mary's house. They are certain God will send an angel, and every door in the prison will swing open before him. If a gust of wind blows: "There's Peter knocking at the door!" If the rain begins to patter: "There's Peter again!" These people are too credulous, too cock-sure. Their faith is not necessarily the genuine article. For even the most devoted Christian, while exercising a faith which must surely bring an answer from God, knows what it is to have lurking just around the corner the question whether perhaps he might be mistaken.

FEBRUARY 26th

He gave him to be head over all things to the church, which is his body, the fulness of him that filleth all in all. Ephesians 1. 22 f.

Do not look at Christ in heaven as an ideal to be arrived at. See Him as God's gift to you. You feel the things of the world pulling you down, but they can no more pull you down than they can pull Him down. You are just as secure in the heavenlies as Christ is. Do you doubt this? There are some yellow flowers on my desk. I did not enter the room and repeat: "There must be some yellow flowers here, there must be some yellow flowers here," and by some kind of auto-suggestion bring them magically into being! No, they were there all the time. I just opened my eyes and looked!

Our faith is no make-believe. It is based on the eternal facts of what God has done in Christ. If we dare to venture our faith upon those facts, the Holy Spirit is here to prove them true. See ourselves there in Christ, and instead of going down, we are sustained by His power.

FEBRUARY 27th

They looked unto him, and were lightened: and their faces shall never be confounded. Psalm 34. 5.

We need to guard against being over-anxious about the subjective side of spiritual experience, and so becoming turned in on ourselves. May I illustrate this from the electric light? You are in a room and it is growing dark. You would like to have the light on in order to read. There is a reading-lamp on the table beside you. What do you do? Do you watch it intently to see if the light will come on? Do you take a cloth and polish the bulb? No, you get up and cross over to the other side of the room where the switch is on the wall, and you turn the current on. You turn your attention to the source of power, and when you have taken the necessary action there, the light comes on here. Dwell always upon what God has done in Christ, and let Him take care of what He will do in you.

FEBRUARY 28th

Rejoice in the Lord alway: again I will say, Rejoice. Philippians 4. 4.

Persecution soon compelled Paul and Barnabas to leave the group of disciples at Antioch in Pisidia and to move on (Acts 13. 50 ff.). What effect had their early departure upon the infant church? Here was a group of new believers, mere babes in Christ. Did they plead with the apostles to remain awhile and care for their spiritual welfare? "If you leave us now we shall be as sheep without a shepherd. Surely one at least of you can remain behind and look after us! The persecution is so intense, we can never get through without your help." Is this how they reasoned? No, instead of such appeals, how amazing is the Scripture record: "And the disciples were filled with joy and with the Holy Ghost"! There was no mourning when Paul and Barnabas moved on, but great gladness, surely because the apostles' departure meant an opportunity for others to hear the Gospel. But not only so. They themselves were provided for; they were filled with the Holy Ghost.

FEBRUARY 29th

I will put my spirit within you, and cause you to walk in my statutes. Ezekiel 36. 27.

Late one summer I stayed at a hill-resort in the home of a mechanic and his wife, both of whom it was my joy to lead to a simple faith in the Saviour. When the time came for me to return to Shanghai, I left with them a Bible.

During the winter the man was in the habit of taking alcohol with his meals, sometimes to excess. Soon, with the return of the cold weather, the wine reappeared on the table, and, as had now become his custom, he bowed his head to give thanks for the meal. But today no words would come! After one or two vain attempts he turned to his wife. "What is wrong?" he asked. "Why cannot we pray today?" The wife took the Bible, but turned the pages in vain, seeking light on the subject. They could find no explanation, and I was far away. "Just drink your wine," she said; but no, he knew he must give thanks, and could not. "Take it away," he exclaimed at length; and then together they asked a blessing on the meal.

When eventually the man was able to visit Shanghai he told me the story. Using an expression familiar in Chinese: "Brother Nee," he said, "Resident Boss wouldn't let me have that drink!" "Very good," I replied, "You always listen to Resident Boss!"

MARCH 1st

He grew up before him as a tender plant, and as a root out of a dry ground. Isaiah 53. 2.

Its roots are the means whereby a plant is nourished, the channel through which its life is derived. No plant can live without a root-system. Equipped with one it may survive in the most unpromising conditions. Isaiah's words suggest that Jesus Himself did not derive His life and strength from outward circumstances. Nor must we. If necessary we must be able to live without the succour of our brethren in Christ. Even with them around us, we live *with* our fellow-members, we do not live *by* them. The secret source of our life is God alone.

But to live thus "out of a dry ground" means something more. It means that nothing merely circumstantial can destroy us. No drought can wither God's tender plants. Amid barren, even hostile conditions His children are equipped to be "more than conquerors". Their life is Christ Himself.

MARCH 2nd

He is able to guard you from stumbling, and to set you before the presence of his glory in exceeding joy. Jude 24.

Here is a wonderful promise for us who have committed our lives into the hands of God. For our pathway towards "the presence of his glory" conceals many pitfalls, and He undertakes to guard us from these. When do we stumble? When, unaware of any obstruction, we strike our foot on something hidden in our path. This verse assures us that God's preserving grace will operate just there, beyond the realm of our consciousness. If we commit ourselves unreservedly to His care, we need not fear the unknown. We shall marvel to see how again and again God preserves us from dangers of which at the time we were wholly ignorant.

MARCH 3rd

The Lord said unto Abram, Get thee out of thy country . . . unto the land that I will show thee. Genesis 12. 1.

This was the second call to Abram, for the first had come when he was in Mesopotamia "before he dwelt in Haran" (Acts 7. 2). Abram had gone forward from Chaldea, but not, it seems, far enough, and it is a solemn thought that no history is recorded of all the days he spent in Haran. But God persisted with His call. We sometimes hope by procrastination to get Him to modify His demands. He will not do that, for He has never abandoned the goal He set before us years ago. If we have let it slip, God has not.

From God's point of view Haran was little advance on Mesopotamia. Abram might be satisfied that he had made a move, but God had called him *to a land*. All true calling is a high calling. Let us content ourselves with no halfway house. The question is not how far we have gone since we started, but whether our hearts are still set on God's goal.

MARCH 4th

Knowing this, that our old man was crucified with him,
that the body of sin might be done away. Romans 6. 6.

For years after my conversion I had been taught to "reckon". But the more I reckoned I was dead to sin, the more alive to sin I clearly was! I simply could not believe myself dead, and I saw no way of producing death. Whenever I sought help from others I was told to read Romans 6. 11, and the more I read Romans 6. 11 and tried to reckon, the further away death was: I could not get at it. In my trouble I said to the Lord, "If I cannot be brought to see this which is so fundamental, I will not preach any more. I *must* be thoroughly clear here." For months I sought and prayed, at times with fasting, but nothing came through.

Then one morning, and it is a morning I shall never forget, as I sat with the Word open and said again, "Lord, open my eyes!" in a flash I *saw* my oneness with Christ. I saw that I was in Him, and that when He died I died. Our old man *was* crucified with Him. Oh it was so real to me! I was carried away with such joy that I longed to go through the streets of Shanghai shouting the news of my great discovery.

MARCH 5th

Wheresoever the gospel shall be preached . . . that also which this woman hath done shall be spoken of.
Mark 14. 9.

Why did the Lord say this? Because the Gospel is meant to produce this kind of action. This is what the Gospel is for. The Gospel is not just to satisfy sinners. Praise God, the sinner has his part. God meets his need and showers him with blessings; but that is, we may say, a blessed by-product of the Gospel and not its primary aim. The Gospel is preached in the first place so that the Lord may be satisfied. But we must remember this, that He will never be satisfied without our "wasting" ourselves upon Him. Have you ever given too much to the Lord? May I tell you something? In divine service the principle of waste is the principle of power. Real usefulness in the hand of God is measured in terms of waste. Our work for Him springs from our ministering to Him, and so do all its fruits.

MARCH 6th

He will tell thee what thou shalt do. Ruth 3. 4.

All Israel were to preserve their family heritage from the days of Joshua to the coming of Christ; hence the return of alienated property in the year of Jubilee. And because continuity of possession required that the original owner have heirs, hence too the law that if a man died leaving a widow and no sons, a near relative must take her and preserve the line. Naomi's case was even worse than that. Widowed, she was now also too old to bear children. How could her late husband's inheritance be restored? Her daughter-in-law Ruth was willing, but an alien. Only the aged Boaz was near enough of kin to help. Would he redeem a foreigner? For Ruth's need was not to be met merely by the purchase of her lands. She must be wed. She must *offer herself* to Boaz.

Without the offering up of ourselves to God, redemption is a sterile, empty thing. Boaz commended Ruth, and rightly, for turning aside from the attractions of younger men so as to fulfil God's law, and a glance at her posterity shows how greatly she was in fact rewarded. Consecration to God pays rich dividends.

MARCH 7th

I know thy tribulation, and thy poverty (but thou art rich). Revelation 2. 9.

As we look around us we cannot but sorrow over a tragic lack in the experience of so many Christians. There is so little about their lives to indicate fulness. They have scarcely sufficient for their own needs, much less anything to spare for others. Why are they so poor? Is it because they do not know what the discipline of the Spirit is designed to lead them to? The Psalmist says, "In pressure thou hast enlarged me" (Psalm 4. 1, J. N. Darby trans.). The object of temporal poverty is eternal enrichment. God never intended that pressure and poverty should issue in nothing. His purpose is that all pressure should lead to enlargement, all poverty to enrichment. God's goal for His people is neither continuous straitness nor continuous poverty. For these are never the end; they are only the means to God's end. Straitness is the pathway to expansion; poverty the pathway to wealth.

MARCH 8th

He said unto me, They are come to pass. I am the
Alpha and the Omega, the beginning and the end.
Revelation 21. 6.

"They are come to pass." At long last God's eternal
purpose has been realized. How has this happened? Why does
Scripture so confidently affirm it? Surely because He is the
Alpha and the Omega. God has begun a work, and He will
perfect it. He can do no other than finish what He has set His
hand to, for it is His very nature to do so. He is not only the
beginning, He is also the end. Hallelujah! Our God is the
Omega as well as the Alpha. This assures us that nothing He
has begun to do in us will be left unfinished. God cannot be
withstood by man's incompetence or by Satan's enmity. Sin
is too much for us, but it is not too much for Him. His Name,
which is His own nature, is our guarantee that He will see His
work in us through to its perfect completion.

MARCH 9th

I press on, if so be that I may apprehend that for which also
I was apprehended by Christ Jesus. Philippians 3. 12.

No master has so many servants as our Master; and
for each He has a suitable employment. Even the little maid
was at hand to testify to Naaman in his need. Many of us
murmur against the position God has given us. We want to
do this, but God puts us into that. We have an ambition to
serve Him here, but His plan for us lies elsewhere. When
faced by such apparent reverses, it is well to remember that

God's purpose for us goes back before our conversion, for His foreknowledge has determined our circumstances even before we were born. God never does a thing suddenly; He has always prepared long, long before. So there is nothing to murmur about, nothing to be proud of, in the calling of God. There is also no one of whom to be jealous, for other people's advantages have nothing to do with us. When we look back over life, we bow and acknowledge that all was prepared by God. So there is no need to fear we have missed something. To have this assurance is true rest.

MARCH 10th

Ye behold me: because I live, ye shall live also. John 14. 19.

John's Gospel reflects everywhere the fact that he is writing for the last days. His burden relates to the life of the eternities and to your right relationship thereto. If you go back to that, he implies, all else will follow. He is not occupied with outward and temporal things; his whole concern is that you should get behind these to the Life. Everything now is in disrepair. Go back to the Life that "came down from heaven", and when you get back there, all that threatens to be lost will be preserved. In a sense John has nothing new to offer us that the other New Testament writers have not given us already. He does not take us further, for the furthest point has already been touched by God. The object of the revelation entrusted to John is to bring people back again to that original purpose, by bringing them into a fresh touch with the risen Lord Himself.

MARCH 11th

She said, The glory is departed from Israel; for the ark of God is taken. 1 Samuel 4. 22.

The ark is taken; but the ark can defend itself, as its captors soon learn to their cost. Because it was primarily a testimony to God's own nature, the ark did something to the Philistines that unholy Israel could not do. God seeks instruments for His glory, but when He cannot find them He does the work Himself, and in so doing takes care of His own testimony. He was willing to let His ark be carried off in order to show to all the world that He will not ally Himself with the cause of His people while there is unholiness with them. God's nature and man's unholiness can never be associated, least of all in His own covenant people.

MARCH 12th

I will give unto thee the keys of the kingdom of heaven. Matthew 16.19.

What qualified Peter to become God's mouthpiece, to open the door of faith first to Jews and then to Gentiles? Surely it was that before Peter spoke he had himself been spoken to; for before he could make use of the keys of the Kingdom he must encounter the demands of that Kingdom upon himself.

What does the term "kingdom" mean? Surely it is the realm of a king, the sphere of his authority. Soon after this, in the Mount of Transfiguration, Peter made his brilliant suggestion which would have provided a place for Moses and Elijah alongside the Lord. But in the *Kingdom* you cannot do that!

You cannot have more than one authority. There can only be one Voice. It was to point this lesson that "while he yet spake" the Father broke in with a rebuke which makes it plain that in the Kingdom everything hangs upon the King Himself speaking and upon our paying heed to His words.

MARCH 13th

One is your Teacher. Matthew 23. 8.

Every Christian "disciple" is by definition a learner, and such he should remain. Set out to be a "teacher" of others and you may over-stretch yourself and create only problems in the minds of simple saints. It is such superiority, born of the overconfidence that we *know*, that effectively closes doors. You must be willing to say, "I do not know; God has not shown me." Profess great knowledge and you invite criticism. But people will not be hard on the worker who adopts the attitude; "If you have something to say to me, I am glad to listen, for I too am a disciple of the Lord." "Be not many teachers, my brethren," says James. My counsel to you therefor is that you remain very long a learner.

MARCH 14th

He is our peace, who made both one, and brake down the middle wall of partition. Ephesians 2. 14.

Like a seven-fold cord the unity of the Spirit binds all believers throughout the world. However diverse be their character or circumstances, provided they possess the vital oneness conferred by His indwelling presence, nothing can possibly separate them. Our unity is not based on our appreciation of the truth of oneness, nor is it based on our separating ourselves from all that would possibly contradict our oneness. It rests securely upon the actual fact of our union with Christ, a union wrought by His Cross and made real in our experience by His indwelling Spirit. No basis of unity could be sounder.

MARCH 15th

Hannah prayed, and said: My heart exulteth in the Lord.
1 Samuel 2. 1.

Speaking naturally, this could have been the saddest moment in Hannah's life, for she was saying goodbye to her young son. Here however we shall find no trace of sorrow or self-pity, but only the expression of a heart overflowing with that unique joy which comes to those who give their all to the Lord. With Hannah, it seems, there was a real exercise of soul in relation to the Lord's interests, and the dearest thing in her life was dedicated to those interests. Before Samuel was born she had made her vow to God. During his infancy she had waited for this day. She weaned Samuel, and now, when the moment came and he was given back to God, she found a new joy such as she had never known before, the joy of the fully committed. Her song, from which centuries later that of Mary was to find inspiration, expresses her triumphant joy.

MARCH 16th

Be it unto me according to thy word. Luke 1. 38.

How essential it was that in the virgin Mary the living Word should find a free way if God's purpose in sending it was to be fulfilled! God spoke, and because her faith responded, His miracle took place. Alas, many of us think it quite enough if we are orthodox in doctrine and give unqualified mental assent to the Word of Truth. But unless that Truth is taking effect inwardly, there may really be no great difference between assent to it and dissent from it. The difference only comes when it begins to play a vital, transforming part in a life. How tragic to have a vast knowledge of the Bible, yet little inward experience of its working. If we are to be of use to God in His great purposes it is essential that we respond not merely with our head but with our heart when His Word comes to us in a present, personal way. Can we echo Mary's prayer?

MARCH 17th

God, whose I am, whom also I serve. Acts 27. 23.

It is a great thing when I discover I am no longer my own but His. If the money in my pocket belongs to me, I have full authority over it. But if it belongs to another who has committed it to me in trust, then I cannot buy what I please with it, and I dare not lose it. How many of us dare not use our time or money or talents as we would because we realize they are the Lord's, not ours? How many of us have such a strong sense that we belong to Another that we dare not squander a dollar of our money, or an hour of our time, or any of our mental or physical powers? We are alive unto God, not unto ourselves. Real Christian life begins with knowing this.

MARCH 18th

Wherefore receive ye one another, even as Christ also received you, to the glory of God. Romans 15. 7.

This passage about differing viewpoints in church life begins with the words "God hath received him" (14. 3) and ends no less strongly with "Christ also received us" (15. 7 mg.). Here is the simple basis of all our fellowship with others. It is that they belong to the Lord and so do we. That is enough. Alas, when you and I meet we generally discuss the points on which we disagree. Instead of dwelling on the Lord whom we have in common, we turn to the negative ground of our differences and stress what is right or wrong in them. Differences abound in the passage before us, but Paul does not tell us who is right. For he is concerned with Christian fellowship, and that does not depend on whether a man's views are right or wrong. The question is not whether he believes exactly what I believe, or has had the same experience as I have had. The sole question is: Has God received him? If so, then I receive him too.

MARCH 19th

I had not known sin, except through the law: for I had not known coveting, except the law had said, Thou shalt not covet. Romans 7. 7.

God knows who I am; He knows that from head to foot I am full of sin; He knows that in the matter of pleasing Him I am weakness incarnate, that I can do nothing. The trouble is I do not know it. I admit that all men are sinners and that therefore I am a sinner, but I imagine I am not such a hopeless sinner as some. While I may agree I am weak, I do not wholly believe it, so God has to use something to convince me of the fact. That is why He gave us the Law, for the more we try to meet its demands, the more our failure becomes manifest. It was through the Law that Paul came really to understand himself—the law which begins "Thou shalt not covet". Whatever might be his experience with the rest of the Law, it was the tenth commandment, which literally translated, is "Thou shalt not desire", that found him out. It brought him face to face with a holy God.

MARCH 20th

God, sending his own Son . . . condemned sin in the flesh: that the ordinances of the law might be fulfilled in us, who walk not after the flesh but after the spirit. Romans 8. 3 f.

What does it mean to walk after the Spirit? It means two things. First, it is not a labour, it is simply a walk. Praise God, the burdensome and fruitless effort I incurred when I sought "after the flesh" to please God gives place now to a quiet and restful dependence on "his working which worketh in me mightily". That is why, in Galatians, Paul contrasts the *works* of the flesh with the *fruit* of the Spirit.

And, secondly, to "walk after" is to follow. It implies subjection, for is He not in the lead? To walk after the Spirit is to be subject to the Spirit in all things. The initiative of life must hereafter be His. There is one thing the man who walks after the Spirit cannot do, and that is run ahead of Him!

MARCH 21st

Behold we call them blessed which endured. James 5. 11.

When God takes it in hand to deal with a man, He does not leave him till He has brought him through to a clear place. In His dealings with Job, God was characteristically thorough. He first allowed all his cattle to be carried off. Then his herds were consumed by fire. Next his sons and daughters died; and he had not yet emerged from his trials when, still protesting, he lay covered with "sore boils from the sole of his foot unto his crown". But a day came when, in his utter subjection to God, Job's protests were silenced and God Himself was free to speak. Then at last his trials issued in final triumph. James refers to this as "the end of the Lord". Clearly therefore what matters is not the number of our trials, but that we reach God's goal through them.

MARCH 22nd

Whosoever shall compel thee to go one mile, go with him twain. Matthew 5. 41.

A brother in South China had a rice field in the middle of the hill. In time of drought he used a water-wheel, worked by a treadmill, to lift water from the irrigation stream into his field. His neighbour had two fields below his, and one night he made a breach in the dividing bank and drained off all his water. When the brother repaired the breach and pumped in more water his neighbour did the same thing again, and this happened three or four times. So he consulted his brethren. "I have tried to be patient and not to retaliate," he said, "but is it right?" After they had prayed together about it, one of them observed, "If we only try to do the right thing, surely we are very poor Christians. We have to do something more than what is right." The brother was much impressed. Next morning he pumped water for the two fields below, and in the afternoon pumped water for his own field. After that the water stayed in his field. His neighbour was so amazed at his action that he began to inquire the reason, until in due course he too found Christ.

"Right or wrong" is the principle of the Gentiles and tax-gatherers (verse 46). Not that, but conformity to Him, must govern my life.

MARCH 23rd

Whether we live, therefore, or die, we are the Lord's.
Romans 14. 8.

Never lay stress on the technical side of Christianity, but always on the fundamental fact that we are Christ's, and that all we do is unto Him. We live "unto the Lord" and we die "unto the Lord". We must never seek to persuade those who differ from us merely to think and act as we do. Our one aim must be to lead them closer to Him. For we are not working for outward correctness, or conformity to certain good things, but for a closer relationship to God Himself. Has a brother views that differ strongly from mine? Let it be my first concern that both he and I are doing what we do as unto the Lord. Where that is our goal, notwithstanding outward divergences, all is well between us. The Lordship of Jesus Christ is the central point of Christianity. If, in truth, He is your Lord and He is my Lord, then He Himself will adjust the other things.

MARCH 24th

Perplexed, yet not unto despair. 2 Corinthians. 4. 8.

From the day I was converted, my sincere ambition was to be a true Christian. Of course I had my own conception of what a Christian should be, and I tried my utmost to be that kind of Christian. A true Christian, I reasoned, should smile from morning to night! If ever he shed a tear, he had ceased to be victorious. He must, too, be unfailingly courageous. The slightest sign of fear would mean he had failed seriously to trust His Lord. He had, in fact, fallen far short of my standard.

But the Christian life, I soon learned, is very different. It is a paradox of power in weakness, joy amid pain, faith triumphing in the presence of doubt. When the Christian is strongest in the Lord he is often most conscious of inability; when he is most courageous he may be profoundly aware of fear within; and when he is most joyful a sense of distress readily breaks upon him again. It is only "the exceeding greatness of the power" that lifts him on high.

MARCH 25th

Pray to thy Father which is in secret, and thy Father which seeth in secret shall recompense thee. Matthew 6. 6.

There is no need for us to devise means to draw attention to our work. God in His sovereign providence can well bear that responsibility. We are trusting God for our living, but what need is there to make it known? I feel repelled when I hear God's servants emphasize the fact that they are living by faith. Do we really believe in God's rule and in His provision? If we do, surely we can trust Him to make our needs known to His saints, and so to order things that they can be met without our proclaiming them. Even should people conclude from our mode of living that we have a private income, and in consequence withhold their gifts, we are not to mind. I would counsel my younger brethren to keep silence not only about their personal needs but about their faith in God, so that they may the better be able to prove Him. The more faith there is, the less talk there will be about it.

MARCH 26th

Go to the sea, and cast a hook, and take up the fish that first cometh up; and when thou hast opened his mouth, thou shalt find a shekel; that take, and give unto them for me and for thee. Matthew 17. 27.

This gracious miracle must surely have been meant to speak as a parable to Peter. *For me, and for thee.* Some have remarked that this incident is the only example of the Lord performing a miracle for Himself. True, but it was only half for Himself, for half was for Peter—and you and I can add, "for me". In that single shekel, meeting by grace the temple-tribute for two men, we have wonderfully set forth the intimate union of the servant with his Lord.

And the miraculous fish? Does it not assure us that, when we are on a right basis with regard to the will of God, the expenses will be found by God Himself? Whenever love has to go further than duty, we can look to Him to meet the charges.

MARCH 27th

The house was filled with the odour of the ointment.
John 12. 3.

By the breaking of that flask for the Lord's sake, the home in Bethany was pervaded with the sweetest fragrance. Something was set free for all to appreciate, and none could be unaware of it. What is the significance of this?

Have you ever met someone who has suffered deeply, and whose experiences have compelled him to find satisfaction in the Lord alone? Then immediately you have become aware of something. Immediately your spiritual senses detect a fragrance—what Paul terms "a sweet savour of Christ". Something has been broken in that life in order to release what is there within of God Himself, and you cannot mistake it. Yes, the odour that filled the house that day in Bethany still fills the Church today. Mary's fragrance never passes.

MARCH 28th

Even though we have known Christ after the flesh, yet now we know him so no more. 2 Corinthians 5. 16.

"On the first day of the week cometh Mary Magdalene early . . . and seeth the stone taken away." But for Mary it was not enough to find the tomb empty; she wanted to see the Lord's body. "I know not where they have laid him!" she cried to the angels. Then, turning, she saw the Lord she knew so well—and she took Him for a stranger. If you doubt the need for divine revelation, consider that!

For here is an important principle. Christ "after the flesh" had been crucified. Knowing Him thus could end only in the vain search for a corpse. Mary, so engaged, saw Jesus standing there but knew Him not. Yet surely her faculties had not altered? No, it was He who had been raised with great power and restored to His glory; and because *He* had changed, the means of knowing Him had necessarily changed too. Only through His speaking to her did Mary know Him, and it is thus alone all revelation comes. This inner clarity of recognition you simply cannot explain in human terms. You just *know*, and that is enough.

Mary wept. Seeking a corpse, she mistook her Lord. Many of us have things to weep about. We reach a deadlock, with no possible way out. But then we hear close at hand a voice say "Mary"—and lo, there before us is the One we thought we had lost!

MARCH 29th

Being therefore by the right hand of God exalted . . . he hath poured forth this. Acts 2. 33.

How can I receive the power of the Spirit for service? Must I labour for it? Must I plead with God for it? Must I afflict my soul by fastings and self denials to merit it? Never! That is not the teaching of Scripture. Think again: How did we receive the forgiveness of our sins? Paul tells us it was according to the riches of His grace, and that that grace was "freely bestowed on us in the Beloved". We did nothing to deserve it. We have our redemption through His blood, that is, on the basis of what *He* has done. What then is Scripture's basis for the outpouring of the Holy Spirit? It is the exaltation of the Lord Jesus. Because Jesus died on the Cross my sins are forgiven; because He is exalted to the throne I am endued with power from on high.

MARCH 30th

It is written, He that glorieth, let him glory in the Lord.
1 Corinthians 1. 31.

Paul speaks somewhere of being "under law to Christ". For you and me this certainly does not mean striving to keep the Law, for we know all too well where that ends! It means instead that we prove His power in us to keep it, and that is something very different. But such dependence on Him can only produce in us a deep humility. Surely it is true that every grace which God produces in me will always make me humble. If I can feel some pride in an accomplishment, then I may be fairly sure that it is the result of my own efforts, for I am unlikely to have pride in what was never done by me at all! It is the one who does the work who gets the glory. God must have all the glory, so He insists on doing all the work. Mine it is to rejoice in what He is doing in me, and to be sure to give to Him the praise.

MARCH 31st

Whatsoever things were written aforetime were written for our learning. Romans 15. 4.

Christianity is built not on precepts alone but on concrete examples. One of God's methods of instruction is through history. It tells us how men knew and did His will, so that by observing their lives we may not only discover that will for ourselves, but learn also how we too may do it. His hand on their lives produced His desire in them, and He bids us take note, so that we may better understand what He designs to do in us.

Is it necessary for a child to be told explicitly how to do

everything? Must each item be specifically permitted or forbidden? Is there not much he can discover simply by watching his parents? We learn more readily by what we see than by what we hear, and the impression upon us is deeper, because of course precepts are abstract, whereas examples tangibly demonstrate their outworking. In principle the ways of God are the same today as in Bible days. He has given us so much history in the Old and New Testaments in order that through patience and comfort of the scriptures we too may have hope.

APRIL 1st

In a great house there are not only vessels of gold and silver, but also of wood and of earth; and some unto honour, and some unto dishonour. If a man therefore purge himself from these, he shall be a vessel unto honour.
2 Timothy 2. 20f.

What distinguishes between these vessels? We note at once that only their materials are specified, not their function. Clearly, in keeping with the greatness of the house, it is not relative usefulness but quality of materials that counts. Gold and silver vessels are less practically useful than wooden furniture or earthenware pots, but God is not here discussing with us what they will be used for; He is judging their value to Himself. In a day of declension God looks beyond mere usefulness to intrinsic worth, and a few ounces of gold may equal in value a whole hall full of wooden benches! In spiritual terms, two different men may utter almost identical words, but the power lies not merely in what they say but in who they are. Balaam and Isaiah both spoke of the Kingdom of Christ, but we know well to which of the two we would turn in personal need.

APRIL 2nd

We are the circumcision, who worship by the Spirit of God, and glory in Christ Jesus, and have no confidence in the flesh. Philippians 3. 3.

Circumcision was a sign that marked out the Jew from the rest of mankind. What is the corresponding mark of our Christian life before men? Is it charity? wisdom? sincerity? zeal? Other men have these. None of them is peculiar to the people of God; but there is one that is. It is a seemly absence of self-confidence! What distinguishes God's own is that their confidence in the flesh is destroyed and they are cast back upon Him. I have known Christians who are so sure they know the will of God that they will not for one moment consider they may be mistaken. I tell you they still lack the supreme sign of the spiritual "circumcision", namely, *no confidence in the flesh.* The spiritual man walks humbly, always aware he may be wrong. He assents gladly to the apocryphal beatitude: Happy are they who realize they may be mistaken!

APRIL 3rd

To this end Christ died, and lived again, that he might be Lord of both the dead and the living. Romans 14. 9.

Paul has been very strong in verse 4, demanding "Who art thou that judgest the servant of another?" (The pronoun "thou" is emphatic in the Greek.) What presumption on our part to judge the Lord's servant who is responsible to Him alone! It is not for you or me to act as lord of the saints and to seek to put them right, as though God could not manage His own servants without us. *We* did not die for them. *I* am lord neither of the dead nor of the living. Dare I, then, take it on myself to regulate other people's lives? Let me be patient with them, even as God has been patient with me. For after all, I trust the working of His Spirit in my own heart. Shall I not equally trust Him to work in the heart of my brother in Christ?

APRIL 4th

How good and how pleasant it is for brethren to dwell together in unity! It is like the precious oil upon the head.
Psalm 133. 1 f.

Psalm 133 is a Song of Ascents, sung three times a year by those going up to worship at Jerusalem. There were all kinds of people on that road, but they had one thing in common: they were all heading for Zion, the abode of God. These men in their great variety were all brothers in unity. How? The illustration explains. It is like the oil.

There is one "holy anointing oil": the Spirit of God Himself. And the flow of oil is down (verse 2) not up! In other words, His anointing is not directly on the members, but upon Christ the Head. The Spirit finds rest and satisfaction in Christ and nowhere else. Hold fast the Head, obey Him in all things, and you will be found walking in step with all who do the same. Rules may be good in society, but the Body has one law: the law of the Spirit of life. Only disregard the anointing spirit, and all is unease; obey Him, and peace fills your heart. Here lies the simplicity of the life of God's children. There is no need for all that questioning!

APRIL 5th

*Let us fetch the ark of the covenant of the Lord out of
Shiloh unto us, that it may save us.* 1 Samuel 4. 3.

To the Israelites the ark of the Lord was the ark of
His covenant. They fancied He would fulfil that covenant
therefore by protecting them from their foes, no matter how
untrue to it they themselves might be. But when God's
children turn from Him with a divided heart He can only
hand them over to defeat. They think He must deliver them
for His glory's sake, but God is more concerned to vindicate
His holy character than to display an empty show of glory.
When a servant of God fails badly, we feel the affair were
better covered up. We pray along such lines therefore, ex-
pecting God, for His own glory, to save from open shame,
even though there be secret defeat. But God's way is the very
reverse of this. He *must* let His people be defeated in the
world's eyes in order to dissociate Himself from their unholiness. He will never cover it up. His glory rests on moral
values, and can better be maintained by their open discomfiture than by the deception of a hollow victory.

APRIL 6th

*Then David arose from the earth, and washed, and
anointed himself, and changed his apparel; and he came
into the house of the Lord, and worshipped.* 2 Samuel
12. 20.

David's son died because of David's sin. True, David
had repented, and being a man of prayer had fasted and
prayed earnestly for his son's life. Nevertheless the child died.

A man of less humble spirit, ignorant of divine discipline, might have been offended and have nursed a grievance against God. David did no such thing. Told of the child's death, he arose at once and worshipped. Sometimes God has to vindicate His own holiness in this way, putting his servants into the very fires of suffering. The great test in that hour is their reaction to His governmental hand. Of course David felt the sorrow keenly—he would scarcely have been human not to. But when at length he realized that this was God's way with him and there was no relenting, he bowed to it and worshipped the will of God. Should such an occasion arise, could we do this? It marked David as a man after God's own heart.

APRIL 7th

Ye shall know the truth, and the truth shall make you free.
John 8. 32.

We must avoid over-spiritualizing what we read in the Word of God. John's new heaven and new earth, for example, are as truly real as the risen Lord is real. To spiritualize away divine things is the desperate expedient of people who do not themselves know that reality. Many of us amass spiritual truth, only, I fear, to build for ourselves with it a false world. We confuse truth and doctrine, but the two are not the same. Doctrine is what is said on earth about the eternal truth. I know well that our word "truth" in the Chinese Bible is *chen-li* (roughly, "reality-doctrine"), but in fact the Greek meaning is *chen* without the *li*—"reality", and the doctrine can come afterwards. The Jesus who said "Ye shall know the truth" Himself embodies all that is true. The mark of our own spiritual maturity will always be that divine things become real to us because *He* is real to us.

APRIL 8th

*For their sakes I sanctify myself, that they themselves also
may be sanctified in truth.* John 17. 19.

One thing is certain, that while there is anything between you and your Lord you can only weaken others. You
cannot uplift them. When they are low, you will bring them
lower. When they feel heavy, your coming will only add to
their heaviness. Instead of being an asset in the fellowship of
God's people you will contribute nothing, but rather detract
from its strength.

But if all is clear between you and Him the reverse is true.
Your very presence can be a benediction, bringing freshness to
those who are jaded and adding life to the whole worship of
the saints, to their prayers and to their praises. Maintain a vital
touch with God yourself, and you may well be used to restore
that same vital touch with Him to those who may seem to
have lost it.

APRIL 9th

*By faith Abraham, being tried, offered up Isaac; yea, he
that had gladly received the promises was offering up his
only begotten son; even he of whom it was said, In Isaac
shall thy seed be called.* Hebrews 11. 17 f.

We can appreciate what Abraham might have said.
He might have argued that, whereas he could understand the
command to expel Ishmael, this new order, not merely to
expel but to slay Isaac, was quite incomprehensible. Ishmael
had been the result of his own misdirected efforts. He could

therefore respect the decision that he be turned out of the home. But Isaac! Isaac was different! He was entirely from God, given not merely to satisfy Abraham's love for a son but to be the means of fulfilling all God's pledged purposes. What could *God* do if Isaac were relinquished?

However, Abraham had learned not to reason. He made no protest at all; he did not even speak of sacrifice; he simply said he would go to Mount Moriah to worship. And true worship is just that—to let go to God all His gifts to us, all our rich experiences and all our hopes in Him, and to find unqualified joy in God Himself.

APRIL 10th

What soldier ever serveth at his own charges? who planteth a vineyard, and eateth not the fruit thereof? 1 Corinthians 9. 7.

It is upon God that our eyes are fixed, it is to Him our material needs are told, and it is He who touches the hearts of His children to meet those needs. Yes, the labourer is worthy of his hire, and the Lord ordained that they who proclaim the gospel shall live of the gospel. But we do well to ask ourselves, Whose labourers are we? If we serve men, by all means let us look to men for our support; but if we are the labourers of God, then though He may meet our needs through our fellow-men, it is to Him we must look and to no other. If the call and commission have come from Him, then the responsibility will be His for all that our obedience to Him involves, and we need never inquire how He is going to discharge it.

APRIL 11th

They have no need to go away; give ye them to eat.
Matthew 14. 16.

Spiritual poverty and spiritual straitness are two of
the greatest problems in the Church. Too many Christians are
so poor they have not sufficient for their own needs. Alas for
any who go to them for help! But poverty is effect, not cause,
and straitness is effect, not cause. The cause of poverty and of
straitness is a lack of the Spirit's discipline. Those who are
wealthy are they, and only they, who have known such
discipline. They have a spiritual history with God, because
they have suffered for the Body's sake. Their sicknesses, their
domestic problems, their adversities, all were for the increase
of Christ in His people. It is they who always have something
to give. Those on the other hand who by-pass such discipline,
choosing instead a life of ease and prosperity—they are the
straitened and the poverty-stricken. The poor and needy come
to them in vain for help. They have no overflow.

APRIL 12th

*That through death he might bring to nought him that had
the power of death, that is the devil.* Hebrews 2. 14.

In the death of Jesus Christ, Satan's power of death
met its match once for all. That death out-dies all other deaths.
Death in Adam does not finish a man, but death in Christ does.
It is a mighty death. In Christ all those who deserve to die have
died, with the result that he who had the power of death no
longer has dominion over them. They are dead; and ashes are

something of which you can never make a fire. Christ's work was not only redemption, it was death's destruction, with all that that means. A house once burned to ashes cannot be burned a second time, for if the first fire has done its work there is nothing for the next to do. For us redeemed sinners who have already died a death in Christ, death itself is passed away. We have become possessors of His incorruptible life.

APRIL 13th

Even so reckon ye yourselves to be dead unto sin but alive unto God in Christ Jesus. Romans 6. 11.

What does reckoning mean? I assure you it is not a form of make-believe! The Greek word "reckoning" means doing accounts, book-keeping. Accounting is the one thing in the world we humans can do correctly. Can an artist paint a landscape with photographic accuracy? Can a historian vouch for the absolute correctness of any record, or the map-maker for the perfect precision of any map? They can make, at best, fair approximations. What then can a man do that is utterly reliable? Arithmetic! There is no scope for error there. One chair plus one chair equals two chairs. That is true in London or Cape Town, New York or Singapore. All the world over and for all time, one plus one equals two.

Can God's affirmations be any less true? Could He conceivably ask me to put down something false in my account book? Of course not! If then He tells us to reckon ourselves dead to sin, it is simply because, in Christ, our death to sin is a fact, one eternally to be relied on.

APRIL 14th

Bind the sacrifice with cords, even unto the horns of the altar. Psalm 118. 27.

For what purpose were burnt offerings placed on the altar of Jehovah? To be wholly consumed to God. While the animal offered might be a bullock or a sheep or a dove according to the offerer's resources, the invariable requirement was that it should be a *whole* burnt offering. For God does not accept less than an utter consecration. Today what the altar signifies is not *doing* for God, but *being* for God. He desires not our work but ourselves. Unlike the sacrifices of the Old Testament, which were immolated in one final act, the New Testament sacrifice is "a living sacrifice" (Romans 12. 1). The meaning of the altar is the offering of our lives to God to be ever consumed, yet ever living: to be ever living, yet ever consumed.

APRIL 15th

A glorious church, not having spot or wrinkle or any such thing. Ephesians 5. 27.

Divine Grace has expressed the eternal purpose of God in the statement that Christ will one day present unto Himself a glorious Church. We note that the water of life and the cleansing of the Word are needed to prepare her, marred as she now is by the Fall, to be presented to Him in glory. For today we stand within the history of fallen man's redemption, and there are defects yet to be remedied, wounds to be healed.

Yet how gracious are the words used of her: "not having spot"—the scars of sin, whose very history is now forgotten; "or wrinkle"—the marks of age and of time lost, for all is now made up and all is new; and "without blemish"—so that Satan or demons or men can find no ground for blame in her. God has leaped in thought over the whole of that history to see His Church in glory, expressing nothing of man's fall, but only the image of His glorified Son.

APRIL 16th

Seeing we have this ministry . . . we faint not. 2 Corinthians 4. 1.

In which do we discern God's highest purpose: in the ministry of gifts or in the ministry of life? For the temporary edification of the churches some may minister by miraculous gifts, but in this passage Paul points us forward to the thing most to be prized, and it is not these but the ministry of life from Christ, a life which comes through death. Not gifts, but the working of the Cross: this is the measure of a man's stature.

For the edification of young churches and the winning of souls, spiritual gifts may take on a special significance, but they are not in themselves a mark of maturity, and they are certainly never something of which to boast. Only the foolish are proud of the words God gives, for has He not shown that He will speak, if need be, through an ass!

APRIL 17th

*Be filled with the Spirit . . . singing and making melody
with your heart to the Lord.* Ephesians 5. 18 f.

Plerousthe, "be being filled", is the expression here
used in relation to the Holy Spirit. "Allow yourselves to be
continually made full." This describes, not a crisis as at Pentecost, but a condition we are to enjoy all the time. And it is not
a matter of spiritual gifts and manifestations outwardly, but
of the personal presence and activity of the Holy Spirit of God
within our spirits—the oil that guarantees the lamp shall burn
on undimmed, long after the midnight hour if need be. Moreover it is not alone a private, individual thing. It is something
we share with other Christians. Paul speaks of making melody
together. Some of us may well find it easier to sing solos than
to keep in time and harmony in a choir, or even in a duet!
Yet the fulness of the Spirit is given to us with this very object, that we shall sing *together* a new song before the throne.

APRIL 18th

*When the vessels were full . . . she said unto her son, Bring
me yet a vessel. And he said unto her, There is not a vessel
more. And the oil stayed.* 2 Kings 4. 6.

The divine almightiness is content to confine itself to
our capacity. The oil of God's Spirit flows according to the
measure man has prepared for God. Divine blessing is subject
to the limits of human channels. "Make this valley full of
ditches," said Elisha on another occasion. "For thus saith the
Lord, Ye shall not see wind, neither shall ye see rain, yet that

valley shall be filled with water. . . . And this is but a light thing in the sight of the Lord: he will also deliver the Moabites into your hand" (3. 16 ff.). Man has not the power to obtain anything more than God has given, but he has the option of taking less. "Ye will not come to me that ye may have life."

APRIL 19th

Jesus said unto him, Again it is written, Thou shalt not tempt the Lord thy God. Matthew 4. 7.

There is a world of difference between tempting God and putting Him to the test. The former is forbidden, the latter welcomed. On the surface the two things may appear the same, but they are not. What distinguishes them is a knowledge of God's will communicated through His Word. Israel and the Egyptians afford an example of this. By venturing into the Red Sea both took the same tremendous risk. It was a risk that led the Israelites to glorious salvation, the Egyptians only to death and ignominy. Why? Because, of the two, Israel alone was acting on a word from God. It was that word they put to the triumphant test.

Or again, consider Paul and his young friend Timothy. Though weak in body the apostle Paul accomplished more in his lifetime than ten strong men. Defying reason he laboured on, proving the sufficiency of God's power. Yet Timothy was not exhorted to imitate him in this. Indeed he was warned to take special care of his health. For him to have essayed what Paul did without a divine command to do so would surely have been to tempt God. But to obey such a command is only to put God's faithfulness to the proof.

APRIL 20th

*Search me, O God . . . and see if there be any way of
wickedness in me.* Psalm 139. 23 f.

      True self-knowledge does not come by our turning
within. Introspection never leads us to clear understanding.
No, it is when there is light coming from God that we see.
I think it is so simple. If we want to satisfy ourselves that our
face is clean, what do we do? Do we feel it carefully all over
with our hands? Of course not. We find a mirror and we
bring it to the light. In that light everything becomes clear.
    You realize, do you not, what it means to say "Search me"?
It certainly does not mean that I search myself. "Search me"
means "*You* search me!" That is the way of illumination. It is
for *God* to come in and search. My true knowledge of self
comes not from my searching myself but from God searching
me.

APRIL 21st

*The law of the Spirit of life in Christ Jesus made me free
from the law of sin and of death.* Romans 8. 2.

      A great burden to merchants in China used to be the
likin tax, a law which none could escape, originating in the
Ch'in Dynasty and operating right down to our own day. It
was an inland tax on the transit of goods, applied throughout
the empire, and having numerous barriers for collection and
officers enjoying very large powers. But a few years ago a
second law came into operation which set aside the *likin* law.
Can you imagine the feelings of relief in those who had

suffered under the old law? Now there was no need to worry; the new law had delivered from the old law. No longer was there need to think beforehand what one would say if one met a *likin* officer!

God delivers us from one law by introducing another. The one bound us inescapably to sin and death; the other liberates us into blessed union with the Spirit of life.

APRIL 22nd

This life is in his Son. He that hath the Son hath the life. 1 John 5. 11 f.

It is a blessed thing to discover the difference between Christian graces and Christ: to know the difference between meekness and Christ, between patience and Christ, between love and Christ. God will not give me humility or patience or holiness or love as separate gifts of His grace. He is not a retailer dispensing grace to us in packets, measuring out some patience to the impatient, some love to the unloving, some meekness to the proud, in quantities that we can take and work on as a kind of capital. He has only one gift to meet all our need: His Son Jesus Christ.

The common idea of holiness is that every item of life should be holy; but that is not holiness, it is the *fruit* of holiness. Holiness is Christ. The Lord Jesus is made over to us to *be* that. So you can put in anything there: love, humility, power, self-control. Today there is a call for patience: He is our patience! Tomorrow the call may be for purity: He is our purity. It does not matter what our personal deficiency, or whether it be a hundred and one different things, He is the answer to our every need.

APRIL 23rd

She said unto her husband, Behold now, I perceive that this is an holy man of God. 2 Kings 4. 9.

What an impression Elisha had already made on that great woman of Shunem! Yet till now he had done no miracle in her home, nor is there any record of his having brought to her some prophetic utterance from God. He had simply got into the way of looking in on them when passing, and sharing a meal. She could not know him very well; yet to her husband she said, "I can see that he is a man of God". It was not apparently what he said or did that conveyed that impression, but who he was. When he came she *sensed* God's presence with him.

What are people sensing about us? We all leave impressions of some kind. Do they register that we are clever? that we are gifted? that *we* are this or that or the other? Elisha's visits had one conscious effect: they left on that home an impression of God Himself.

APRIL 24th

I therefore, the prisoner in the Lord, beseech you to walk worthily of the calling wherewith ye were called. Ephesians 4. 1.

Has it dawned upon me yet that *the Spirit of God within me is a Person*? I am but an earthen vessel, but in that vessel I carry a treasure of unspeakable worth, even the Lord of glory. All the worry and fret of God's children would end if their eyes were opened to the wealth of resources they carry with them, resources sufficient for every demand they will ever meet. All their flippancy too would cease if they realized the greatness of the treasure hidden in their hearts. If you have only a dollar in your pocket you can march gaily along the street knowing that it matters little if you lose your money, for there is not much at stake. But if the sum you carry is five thousand dollars, the position is vastly different, and your whole demeanour will be different too. There will be great gladness in your heart, but no careless jaunting along the road; and once in a while you will slacken your pace and, slipping your hand into your pocket, you will quietly finger your treasure again, and then with joyful solemnity continue on your way. Yes, I say it with the utmost reverence: You who have been born again of the Spirit of God—you carry God in your heart!

APRIL 25th

There they dwelt with the king for his work. 1 Chronicles 4. 23.

David had many mighty men. Some were generals, others gatekeepers, according as the king assigned them their tasks. We must be willing to be either generals or gatekeepers, allocated to our parts just as God wills and not as we choose. If you are a Christian, God has marked out a pathway for you —a "course" the apostle terms it in 2 Timothy 4. 7. For not Paul's path only but the path of every child of God has been clearly marked out by Him. It is of supreme importance therefore that each should know and walk in his God-appointed course. "Lord, I give myself to Thee with this desire alone, to be led onward in the path Thou hast ordained." That is true consecration. If at the close of a life we can say with Paul: "I have finished my course," we are blessed indeed. For we have only one life to live down here, and there could be nothing more tragic than to come to its end knowing the course we had taken to have been a wrong one.

APRIL 26th

The path of the righteous is as the shining light, that shineth more and more unto the perfect day. Proverbs 4. 18.

In spite of the examples of Solomon and several other kings, we need not assume that a man's last days should be days of spiritual decline. Think of Jacob after his return to Canaan. He who had always been so restless settled down quietly in the land. There, in the sphere of his own family, he underwent many sorrows and disappointments, yet in them all he displayed a patience and a concern for others quite foreign to the selfish character of his earlier years. Or see him again in Egypt, as father of its mighty ruler Joseph. Whereas the Jacob of former days would eagerly have grasped at this new opportunity for self-advancement, the mellow old man he now was seemed quietly content to remain in the background. The mature prophetic blessings of such a man afford a fitting climax to the book of Genesis.

APRIL 27th

Here is the patience and the faith of the saints. Revelation 13. 10.

There are those who cry "How long?" who find it hard to exercise patience any more. But it is significant that right at the start of this book which deals with judgment,

John should describe himself as "your brother and partaker with you in the tribulation and kingdom and patience which are in Jesus". This book of Revelation brings us to the point where God at length sets aside patience and executes judgment. Patience is only called for while judgment lies yet in the future. Once it has begun there is no more need of patience. But that moment has not yet come, and like John we still live in the time when patience is needed. It is so easy to want to take up the sword against oppression and evil, but even the martyred saints are told to wait the completion of their number (6. 10 f.). God will never justify impatience. He Himself is long suffering. Let us display true faith in Him by availing ourselves of His patience.

APRIL 28th

Now hath God set the members each one of them in the body, even as it pleased him. 1 Corinthians 12. 18.

Tell me, which is the better member, the foot or the hand? There is, when you come to think of it, no way of comparing them. Their function in the human body is quite different, and each is equally needed there. And yet many minimize God's calling. Because they cannot be the special member they admire, they decline to take their place at all. This is exactly the situation described in Jesus' parable of the men with the talents in Matthew chapter 25. There was a servant with five talents, and another with two, but the whole emphasis of the parable is on the one-talent man. The danger is of the one-talent brother burying his talent. "Since I cannot occupy a place of prominence," he asks himself, "does it matter therefore whether I occupy any place at all?" It most certainly does! For the parable teaches that if two can grow into four, one can grow into two. It is by functioning that we discover life. The Church's life is hampered and impoverished by the holding back of the one-talent members.

APRIL 29th

My flesh and my heart faileth: but God is the strength of my heart and my portion for ever. Psalm 73. 26.

A brother I know was called to go on a preaching tour of some months. His wife, to whom he was very attached, was in poor health at the time. A friend had sent me with a last-minute letter to him, and as I came in sight of his house, unseen by him, I observed him come out, walk a little distance, then stop, and after a little hesitation begin slowly to return. I did not wait, but sensing his conflict of spirit I went ahead to the river-boat by another route. On his arrival there I handed him the letter with the words, "May the Lord bless you," and his answer revealed that he was quite at peace. When after some months he came back from the tour I alluded to the incident. "Yes," he confessed, "as I stood there, I felt I *could* not leave her and the children with no help and very little money, but as I was retracing my steps the verse came to me: 'No man, having put his hand to the plough, and looking back, is fit for the kingdom of God.' So I turned again and went down to the boat." To hold on to the plough while wiping our tears—that is Christianity.

APRIL 30th

Fear not ye, neither be dismayed . . . for the battle is not yours but God's. 2 Chronicles 20. 15.

Fight to *get* the victory, and you have lost the battle at the very outset. Your discomfiture as a Christian starts the moment you begin to reckon that *you* must win. Suppose Satan sets out to assault you in your home or in your business. Difficulties mount up, misunderstandings arise, a situation you can neither deal with nor escape threatens to overwhelm you. You pray, you fast, you struggle and resist for days, but nothing happens. Why? You are trying to fight *into* victory, and in doing so are relinquishing the very ground that is yours. For in the person of Jesus Christ God has already conquered. Victory is ours *because it is His*. He has given us His victory to hold. Satan *is* a defeated foe. It needs but a breath from the Lord to finish him off, and here you are trying to raise a hurricane! What then is the secret? Simply look up and praise Him. "Thy victory, Lord, is all-inclusive. I praise Thee it covers this situation too!" Then be at rest in a triumph already secured for you by God.

MAY 1st

They presumed to go up to the top of the mountain: nevertheless the ark of the covenant of the Lord, and Moses, departed not out of the camp. Then the Amalekite came down, and the Canaanite . . . and smote them. Numbers 14. 44 f.

On hearing the report the ten spies brought back to Kadesh-Barnea, Israel had rebelled and refused to enter Canaan. Then, when condemned by God to the choice they had made, they rebelled once more, and insisted now on going ahead in their own strength. They ignored Moses, and the ark of testimony which till now had gone before them in their journeyings. This was their undoing. Not only were they completely routed by their foes; after this incident there is no history of the ark for the 38 years that follow. How striking this is! When we wilfully go our own way, we have no testimony to the faithfulness of God's direction. By our headstrong action we have deprived ourselves of the unique privilege of being led.

MAY 2nd

So he caused the ark of the Lord to compass the city.
Joshua. 6. 11.

Mention here of the ark alone makes it appear as though the writer were ignoring the whole company of people who marched in faith round those walls. But of course it was the ark that really mattered. This stronghold of Jericho was not demolished by the march of the Israelites alone. As we know only too well, we may walk round our own Jerichos a thousand times, and still find nothing happens. Israel's strength lay in the fact that the ark of the testimony was among them. They carried with them the evidence of God's faithfulness hitherto. It was not on the basis of their present effort that they faced their foes, but on the fact of what their God had already done. For us today God's "ark of testimony" is the person of His risen Son. Make Him central, go forth proclaiming His resurrection, and God will bring down those walls.

MAY 3rd

After these things I heard as it were a great voice of a great multitude in heaven, saying, Hallelujah; Salvation, and glory, and power, belong to our God. Revelation 19. 1.

This, the first Hallelujah in the book of Revelation, is provoked by the downfall of a city which is again and again described as "great". Why does heaven so exult at the overthrow of Babylon? Because Babylon embodies the spirit of empty show and pretence. Israel's first recorded sin after entering Canaan was the taking of a Babylonish garment. Achan coveted Babylon's grand style; he wanted to look well. And the first sin recorded in the early Church was similar; an attempt on the part of Ananias and his wife Sapphira to win man's esteem by appearing more self-sacrificing than they in fact were. They too wanted to look well. How readily in the churches today do we put on an act to impress others and establish for ourselves a place of repute and acclaim! This is the principle of Babylon the whore, and it is abominable to God.

MAY 4th

If ye know these things, blessed are ye if ye do them. John 13. 17.

I knew of an old Japanese Christian woman who was disturbed by a thief who broke into her house. She saw he was desperately hungry, and in her simple but practical faith in the Lord, she cooked the man a meal; then ended by offering him her keys. He was utterly shamed by her action, and God spoke to him. Through her testimony, that man is a brother in Christ today.

Too many Christians have all the doctrine in their heads, but live lives that contradict it. They know, for example, all about Ephesians 1-3, but they neglect the practical commands of chapters 4-6: put away falsehood; be kind; forgive; subject yourselves to one another; love your wives; obey your masters; forbear threatening; pray! It were better to have no doctrine at all than to be a contradiction. Has God commanded something? Then cast yourself on Him for help— and do it!

MAY 5th

Having therefore, brethren, boldness to enter into the holy place by the blood of Jesus . . . let us draw near. Hebrews 10. 19 ff.

At my first approach to God I was made nigh by the blood of Christ, and to continue in that new relationship I come through the blood every time. It is not that I was saved on one basis and that I now maintain my fellowship with Him on another. You say, "That is very simple; it is the A.B.C. of the Gospel." Yes, but the trouble with many of us is that we have moved away from the A.B.C. We have thought we had progressed and so could dispense with it, but one can never do so.

For it is the one secure way to Him. Of course, were it conceivably possible for the precious blood to suffer any change, the basis of our approach to God might be less trustworthy. But the blood of Christ has never changed and never will. God looks upon it, and is satisfied. Our approach to Him is therefore always in boldness.

MAY 6th

If any man hath not the Spirit of Christ, he is none of his.
Romans 8. 9.

God's gift to you of the Holy Spirit depends upon the exaltation of His Son to heaven and upon this alone. Is it possible then that the Lord Jesus has been glorified and you who have believed have not received the Spirit? Yet some are confused about this. A young man I knew in Shanghai, having heard with new understanding about the glorified Christ and His outpoured Spirit, went home and began to pray earnestly: "Lord, I believe. I want Thy Holy Spirit's power. Seeing Thou, Lord, hast been glorified, pour out now Thy Spirit on me!" Then he paused, and corrected himself: "Oh no, Lord, that's all wrong!" and he began to pray again: "We are in a life-partnership, Thou, Lord Jesus, and I, and the Father has promised us two things: glory for Thee, and the Spirit for me. Thou hast received the glory; it is unthinkable, therefore, that I have not received the Spirit. Thank you, Lord, for this wonderful gift!"

MAY 7th

Joseph brought in Jacob his father, and set him before Pharaoh: and Jacob blessed Pharaoh. Genesis 47. 7.

Twice over we are told that Jacob blessed Pharaoh. How could this crippled old refugee dare to bestow a blessing on the greatest world monarch of his time? For to Jacob, such an ambition was a thing of the past. In his own eyes now he was nothing.

Yes, but God was with him! Before entering Egypt he had made sure of that. Abraham, a much greater man than he, had come down to Egypt and had sinned. So even though his own son Joseph was here, Jacob had paused at Beer-sheba to offer sacrifices to his father's God, thus putting the decision back in God's hands. And the divine re-assurance had come: "I will go down with thee." And so here he was, broken in the old strength that had grasped at blessings for himself, but mighty enough in spiritual power to bless a monarch.

MAY 8th

The Lord seeth not as man seeth; for man looketh on the outward appearance, but the Lord looketh on the heart.
1 Samuel 16. 7.

Saul was of striking stature. "From his shoulders and upward he was higher than any of the people." No wonder Israel acclaimed him: they could all see his head. Yet how often does the head of man stand in the way of the will of God! It seems David understood this—David the man after God's own heart, who time and again set human reason aside and acted instead in simple faith. Confronted with Goliath (whose head was even more prominent than Saul's) he declined helmet and mail and went out against him with but a sling. One well-aimed stone from this, lodged in the giant's brow, brought him down. That day marked David out as Israel's king.

There are Christians today who are ruled by their head. Historically our Goliath was overthrown at Calvary, but spiritually Saul lives on in us still. Yet let us not look within. Saul is not our foe; his days are numbered. But if David of the shepherd heart is to reign, it is our attitude to the uncircumcized Philistine that must be clear. What he stands for must be confronted by each of us, and it must go.

MAY 9th

For this cause shall a man leave his father and mother, and
shall cleave to his wife: and the twain shall become one
flesh. Matthew 19. 5.

Eve was one and alone; and she was made absolutely
for Adam. This makes her unusual, even unique, among the
women of the Old Testament who may be felt to be types of
the Church. In each of them some aspect of the Church's redemption is depicted. We see her presented to the bridegroom
(Rebekah), chosen from among the Gentiles (Asenath), passing
through the wilderness (Zipporah), receiving her inheritance
in the land (Achsah), altogether dependent upon her kinsman-
redeemer (Ruth), and militant for her lord (Abigail). Yet none
is so instructive as Eve. For they all succeed the Fall, but she, in
that blessed period before sin entered, shows us the Church
fulfilling all God's desire for her in union with His Son. Eve
first came forth from Adam, to be then brought back to him
as his help-meet. From one there became two; from those two
there was again one. This is the mystery of the Church, that in
her, what is altogether from Christ returns once more to Him.

MAY 10th

By faith he forsook Egypt, not fearing the wrath of the
king: for he endured as seeing him who is invisible.
Hebrews 11. 27.

In the preparation of His servants God is most
thorough. Consider the lessons Moses learned to qualify him
to lead Israel out of Egypt. He began life by being himself
drawn out of the water, an experience kept always before him
by his very name of Moses. This, his first exodus, was itself a

triumph over death. Next he must make a deliberate choice to abandon the palace of Pharaoh, declaring thus by another exodus that the world too had no dominion over him. There followed a descent into obscurity, where for forty long years the gifted man he was remained lost to view. Only after that, at the Burning Bush, did the call come again to him to make one more exodus, now from weakness and banishment to prominence and new power as Israel's deliverer. For it was only a man so proved, in whom self, the world and death had been undone, that God could use to play the leading role in Israel's own deliverance.

MAY 11th

I am come down from heaven, not to do mine own will, but the will of him that sent me. John 6. 38.

God's will for me must not be made subject to my own temperament. When we know a man's make-up it is often all too easy to guess what "guidance" he will get, because his natural proclivities intrude so subtly upon the leading of God. Too much so-called guidance among us is little more than personal bias. A timid brother is "guided" to take a back seat. A forward brother is "guided" to take a front seat. Each claims to be led of the Lord. Is he? Or is his temperament ruling him? The pure will of God demands of me that what I am temperamentally shall be set aside. I should be so Spirit-filled that the man beside me cannot foresee, on grounds of my temperament alone, how God will lead me. Oh let me beware of slanting the will of God in the direction of my own natural leanings! Even the Lord Jesus, whose own will was surely faultless, nevertheless set it aside in favour of the Father's who sent Him. If He should do that, how much more must I!

MAY 12th

*For hereunto were ye called: because Christ also suffered
for you, leaving you an example, that ye should follow his
steps.* 1 Peter 2. 21.

How tempted we Christians are to seek spiritual experiences for their own sake! This is wrong. The Bible offers
us no experience as a thing in itself apart. What God has done
in His grace is to include us in Christ. In dealing with Christ
He has dealt with the Christian; in dealing with the Head He
has dealt with all the members. Thus we are quite wrong to
think we can possess anything of the spiritual life in ourselves
merely, and apart from Christ. God does not intend that we
should acquire from Him something exclusively personal, and
He is unwilling to effect anything of the kind in you and me.
All true Christian experience is first of all true in Christ.
What we call "our" experience is only our entering into His
history and His experience. It is the Vine that gives character
to the branches.

MAY 13th

*Moses said unto the people, Fear ye not, stand still, and see
the salvation of the Lord which He will work for you today.*
Exodus 14. 13.

It is always good to have mountains to right and left,
an enemy behind and the sea in front, for then faith has its
opportunity. One great hindrance to faith is lack of need. If
God blesses you with need He will bless you with faith, and
faith works best in really desperate need. Faith, we are told,
can remove a mountain. Nothing is said about ant-hills! You

will find no record in Scripture of the Lord healing a mild headache. No, He deals with the impossible cases. The trouble is that when God gives us a chance to exercise faith, you and I so often cast it aside.

There is little sense in believing if at the same time you provide yourself with an alternative way out! Faith works most convincingly when there is none. Pray boldly therefore to be shut up, as Israel was, to the Sea. Then, to unbelief's question "Can God?", you can dare to affirm as your personal confession: "He is able."

MAY 14th

Thus shall ye eat it; with your loins girded, your shoes on your feet, and your staff in your hand: and ye shall eat it in haste: it is the Lord's passover. Exodus 12. 11.

The shed blood was for God. It was sprinkled on the outside of the house where it would not even be seen by the first-born son within, he who by its virtue was being delivered. No, the blood was for God to see, and He promised that when He saw it He would pass over the house. God's need is met in the blood, but our need is provided for in the festival meal. Within the house we need to feed on the flesh of that Lamb whose blood protects us. It is by so feeding that we are strengthened for the pilgrim journey ahead. The passover meal was not for those who would settle down in Egypt, even protected there by sacrificial blood. It was for them whose manifest purpose was to move out and on with God. And so it is with us. Our needs we find met in Christ as we partake of Him. But remember, we do so always in readiness for onward movement in the will of God.

MAY 15th

*Who . . . tasted the good word of God, and the powers of
the age to come.* Hebrews 6. 5.

The kingdom of God is at once present and to come
(Matthew 6. 10 and 12. 28). As to time it lies ahead of us; as to
experience it is ours today. God intends us to enjoy foretastes
here and now of the powers of the future age. All that will be
true then universally should be the Church's experience in
some real measure now, for all is hers. What is the use of
merely knowing all about conditions in the kingdom: the rest,
the life eternal, the everlasting covenant, the overthrow of
Satan, the authority of God and of His Christ? These are not
future prospects alone, but powers to be tasted here and now.
To taste means to eat a little. It is the preliminary to a feast.
We cannot yet feast on all the good things of the kingdom,
but we should be savouring them. Where spiritual resources
are in demand, let us not live by the present alone. The powers
of the age to come are ours.

MAY 16th

*Buy the truth, and sell it not; yea wisdom and instruction
and understanding.* Proverbs 23. 23.

Lies have no price upon them. They are cheap and
they abound everywhere. But for the truth there is always a
price to pay. First there is the price of humility, for it is to the
meek that light is given from God. If we are not prepared to
buy the truth at the cost of our own humbling we shall not

receive it. Then there is the price of patience. Quick verdicts and impatient decisions have little to do with the divine light which is given to those who will wait upon God and wait for God. And supremely, there is the price of obedience. "If any man willeth to do his will, he shall know." Unquestioning obedience is essential if we would know God's will and God's ways. Is our faith the cheap, easy kind that pays no price? Or are we prepared to have it founded on the truth of God, however great to us the cost of coming by that truth?

MAY 17th

We which have believed do enter into that rest. Hebrews 4. 3.

Rest follows work. In the fullest sense, rest is only possible when the work is completed to a point of satisfaction. It is no trifling matter that God rested after those six days of creation. How, we may ask, could He—this God of purpose, this God of abounding life—come to rest? Genesis 1. 31 gives us the reason: "God saw everything that he had made, and behold, it was very good." He had accomplished something which rejoiced His heart. The good pleasure of His will had been realized, its goal attained. In resting He proclaimed His approval.

Today God invites us to share with Him His rest in Christ. Another work is accomplished, a new creation secured. His good pleasure has been realized, and no fuller realization is necessary or possible. We enter into God's rest when, ceasing from our own strivings, we find all our satisfaction in Christ.

MAY 18th

There were some that had indignation among themselves,
saying, To what purpose hath this waste of the ointment
been made? Mark 14. 4.

What is waste? Waste means, among other things, giving more than is necessary. If a dollar will do and you give ten, it is a waste. If fifty grammes will do and you give a kilogram, it is a waste. If three days will suffice to finish a task well enough and you lavish five days or a week on it, it is a waste. Waste means that you give something too much for something too little. If someone is receiving more than he is considered to be worth, then that is waste. Even the twelve thought this woman's sacrifice excessive. To Judas of course, who had never called Jesus "Lord", everything poured out upon Him was a waste, just as in the world's estimation today our giving ourselves to the service of God is counted sheer waste. But when once our eyes have been opened to the real worth of our Lord Jesus, nothing is too good for Him.

MAY 19th

I Jesus have sent mine angel to testify unto you these things
for the churches. I am the root and the offspring of David,
the bright, the morning star. Revelation 22. 16.

The book of the Revelation is the unveiling, the *apokalupsis*, of Jesus Christ. It draws aside the curtain to reveal Him. Its object is not primarily to enlighten us regarding coming events—the antichrist, the supposed revival of the Roman empire, the rapture of the saints, the millennial kingdom or the final downfall of Satan. John's remedy for our ills is not a matter of so many seals and trumpets and vials. It is not in fact designed to satisfy our intellectual curiosity at all, but to meet our spiritual need by revealing Christ Jesus Himself in fulness, that we may know Him. For Christ is the answer to all our questions. Get clear first about Him, and we shall know all we need to know about "things to come". He is the risen and victorious King of kings. All the events that follow are the outcome of His being that.

MAY 20th

Know ye not, that to whom ye present yourselves as servants unto obedience, his servants ye are whom ye obey.
Romans 6. 16.

The word here rendered "servant" really signifies a bondservant or slave. The distinction is important to us, for this word is used several times in the second half of Romans 6, where Paul writes of our usefulness to God. What is the difference between a servant and a slave? A servant may serve another, but the ownership does not pass to that other. If he likes his master he can serve him, but if he does not, he can give in his notice and seek another master. Not so is it with the slave. He is not merely another man's servant; he is his possession. How did I become the slave of the Lord? On His part He bought me at the price of His life laid down; on my part I presented myself freely and completely to Him. Let us not overlook that second statement. By right of redemption I am God's property, but if I would be useful as His slave, I must willingly give myself to Him for this. He will never compel me.

MAY 21st

To know the love of Christ which passeth knowledge, that ye may be filled unto all the fulness of God. Ephesians 3. 19.

While He was on earth Jesus was Himself the vessel of divine life. When men touched Him they touched God; when they saw Him they saw God. In Him bodily there dwelt all the fulness of the Godhead. This was the Father's pleasure (Colossians 1. 19; 2. 9).

Today what do they see? We who believe possess that life. We are said to have received of His fulness. When men meet us do they meet the surpassing love of Christ? When they touch us, do they touch something of God?

MAY 22nd

We which live are alway delivered unto death for Jesus' sake, that the life also of Jesus may be manifested in our mortal flesh. 2 Corinthians 4. 11.

What does this mean? It simply means that I will act only while leaning on God. I will find no sufficiency in myself. I will take no step just because I have inherited the power to do so. With the forbidden fruit Adam became possessed of an inherent power to act, but a power that played right into Satan's hands. You lose that power when you come to know the Lord. You live now by the life of Another, drawing everything from Him.

Oh, my friends, I think we all know ourselves in measure, but many a time we do not truly tremble at ourselves. We may say in a manner of courtesy to God, "If He does not want it, I cannot do it", but in reality we are pretty sure we can do it quite well ourselves! Too often we have been caused to decide, to act, to have power apart from Him. The Christ we manifest is too small because in ourselves we have grown too big. May God forgive us!

MAY 23rd

O the depth of the riches both of the wisdom and the know-ledge of God! How unsearchable are his judgments, and his ways past tracing out. Romans 11. 33.

Once and again amid the doctrinal unfoldings of God's Word we encounter sudden outbursts of worship from the full hearts of His servants. The apostle Paul displays a happy knack of doing this. In Romans 1 he breaks the flow of his grim exposure of human corruption with a cry of praise to God the Creator, "who is blessed for ever" (verse 25), adding to it his own personal "Amen". Again in Chapter 9 he inter-rupts his discourse on Israel's historic advantages with a closely similar cry acclaiming Christ "over all, God blessed for ever. Amen." And here at the end of Chapter 11 we find the same gay spontaneity. Speaking of God's mercy to the Gentiles and of what their response will be, he concludes: "God hath shut up all unto disobedience that He might have mercy upon all," (11. 32), and logically this is followed by Chapter 12. 1, "I beseech you therefore, brethren, by the mercies of God . . .". But once more Paul interrupts himself, and our text occupies the gap. He cannot suppress his feelings: "for of him, and through him, and unto him, are all things. To him be the glory for ever. Amen." This kind of interruption creates no problem for God!

MAY 24th

That which they have need of . . . let it be given them day by day without fail. Ezra 6. 9.

If we really trust God, we shall expect to bear unaided the spiritual burden both of our own needs and of those of the work. We must not secretly hope for support from some human source. Our faith is not to be in God plus man, but in God alone. If brethren show their love, thank God; but if they do not, let us thank Him still. For God's servant to have one eye on Him and one eye on other men is a shameful thing, unworthy of any Christian. To profess trust in God, yet to turn to the brethren for supplies, is to bring only disgrace on His name. Our living by faith must be transparently real, and never deteriorate into a living charity. Yes, in all material things we dare to be utterly independent of men, because we dare to believe utterly in God. We have cast away all other hope, because we have unbounded hope in Him.

MAY 25th

Sin shall not have dominion over you: for you are not under the law, but under grace. Romans 6. 14.

When God's light first shines into my heart my one cry is for forgiveness, for I realize I have committed sins before Him; but when once I have received forgiveness of sins I make a new discovery, namely, that I still have the nature of a sinner. There is an inward inclination to sin, a power of sin compelling me. When that power breaks out I commit sins. I may seek and receive forgiveness, but then I sin once more.

So life pursues a vicious circle of sinning and being forgiven and sinning again. I appreciate the blessed fact of God's pardon, but I desperately want something more. I rejoice in the forgiveness for what I have done, but I need also deliverance from what I am. I need the Cross of Christ to strike at the root of my capacity to sin. The Blood of Christ has dealt with my sins, but only the power of His death and resurrection is sufficient to deal with me.

MAY 26th

Ye are all one man in Christ Jesus. Galatians 3. 28.

To us who believe, the Cross of Christ is central; central to all time because central to the whole work of God. We praise God for making this fact clear to our hearts. Moreover, it is central also to our lives. But we must remember that in its work for the individual sinner the Cross was, and is, a means to an end, never an end in itself. The divine end to which it leads is the one new man in Christ.

Salvation, personal holiness, victorious living, walking after the Spirit: all these most precious fruits of redemption are ours to enjoy, but they are not meant to apply to us merely as so many myriads of separate units, scattered over this earth for God. Their values are intended to go further than that. Each is ours in terms of the Body of Christ. It may be true that the children of Abraham are as the stars in multitude. Nevertheless as Christians God would have us see ourselves not as men but as a Man. The goal of the divine thought is in fact one heavenly Man, not a host of little men.

MAY 27th

Let us hold fast the confession of our hope that it waver not;
for he is faithful that promised. Hebrews 10. 23.

Nothing so satisfies God as our confession of Him. Jesus often said "I am". He loves to hear us say "Thou art". We do it far too little. When everything goes wrong and all is confusion, don't pray! Confess "Thou art Lord!" Today, when the world is in turmoil, stand and proclaim that Jesus is King of kings and Lord of lords. He loves to hear us say what we *know*.

And Satan too—he trembles when he hears the saints make positive declarations of fact. The name of Jesus is above every other name. Declare it! Say it to the enemy. The word of our testimony will often prove effective where prayer fails to bring results. We are told to speak directly to the mountain and say "Be thou removed!"

MAY 28th

All things whatsoever ye pray and ask for, believe that ye
have received them, and ye shall have them. Mark 11. 24.

Faith is your acceptance of God's fact. Had you thought of this? True faith always has its roots in the past. What relates to the future is hope rather than faith, though of course the two are closely interlinked. In these words of Jesus you are assured that, if you believe you already *have received* your requests (that is, of course, in Him), then "you shall have them". To believe that you *may* get something, or that you *can* get it, or even that you *will* get it, is not faith in the sense meant here. This is faith: to believe that you have already got it. Such faith does not say "God can" or "God may" or "God will" or "God must". "God", it affirms, "*has done it*". The Christian life is lived progressively, as it is entered initially, by faith in divine fact.

MAY 29th

We wronged no man, we corrupted no man, we took advantage of no man. 2 Corinthians 7. 2.

The Lord's servants should be willing to be taken advantage of, but on no account should they ever take advantage of others. It is a shameful thing to profess trust in God and yet to play the role of a pauper, disclosing one's need and provoking others to pity. He who really sees the glory of God, and his own glorious position as one of His workmen, can well afford to be independent of others—independent, yes, and even liberal. It is quite in order for us to enjoy the hospitality of our brethren for a while, but we should most rigidly guard against taking liberties in such trifles as a night's lodging, an odd meal, the use of light or coal or household goods, or even a daily paper. Nothing reveals smallness of character so readily as the taking of petty advantages. Am I a beggar seeking alms? Or am I a servant of the living God?

MAY 30th

The second time the cock crew. And Peter called to mind the word, how that Jesus said unto him, Before the cock crow twice, thou shalt deny me thrice. And when he thought thereon, he wept. Mark 14. 72.

We may think we are as good as Peter—possibly even a little better, for he was tempted and fell. Yes, but was he not better in his fall than many who never do so? He denied —but he was not insensitive. He called to mind the Lord's word; and when he thought thereon, *he wept.* The Christian to whom God's word has no power to appeal is a poor Christian, unworthy of the name. For His word is His instrument of cleansing and renewal. If we only realize this and let it do its work, though we may indeed fail, we shall not long remain unaware that we have done so.

MAY 31st

Ye were redeemed . . . with precious blood, as of a lamb without blemish and without spot, even the blood of Christ. 1 Peter 1. 18 f.

Sin poses for God a threefold problem. Entering as disobedience, it creates first of all an estrangement between God and man. God can no longer have fellowship with mankind, for there is something now which hinders. Thus it is first of all God who says, "They are all under sin" (Romans 3. 9). Then secondly, that sin in man which constitutes a barrier to his fellowship with God gives rise in him to a sense of guilt. Here it is the man himself who, with the help of his awakened conscience, says "I have sinned" (Luke 15. 18). Nor is this all, for sin also provides Satan with his ground of accusation in our hearts, so that thirdly, it is the Accuser of the brethren (Revelation 12. 10) who now says, in effect, "You have sinned."

To redeem us, therefore, and to bring us back to the purpose of God, the Lord Jesus had to do something about these three questions of sin and of guilt and of Satan's charge against us. His precious Blood, shed for many, was alone sufficient to meet this problem, satisfying God, covering our sinfulness, and wholly discomfiting our great Accuser.

JUNE 1st

His branches shall spread, and his beauty shall be as the olive tree, and his smell as Lebanon. Hosea 14. 6.

Hosea surely knew something of the scent of coni-fers. From Lebanon he paints us a picture of what the Christian life should be in its effect on others. The impression of Christ it gives should penetrate everywhere like pine-fragrance. A man's sense of smell is the most delicate of his senses. Through it he receives impressions of what is beyond reach of touch, and even out of sight altogether. Nor need anything be said. For where there is fragrance the effect is everywhere, pervad-ing all. You cannot hide it. So does one whose roots are in Christ shed forth, like the cedar, a sweet savour of Him who is his unseen source of life. We carry with us the unassuming beauty of the Holy Spirit, as figured in the olive, and the effect is to make people aware only of a fragrant influence of Christ. He cannot be hid.

JUNE 2nd

They that dwell under his shadow shall return; they shall revive as the corn and blossom as the vine. Hosea 14. 7.

Who ever gave much thought to vine-blossom! It is in fact one of the shortest-lived of flowers, scarcely noticed before it is gone and has already turned to fruit. In nature we may recognize three types of plants: those which flower but bear no fruit at all; those, such as the peach, which are re-markable both for their blossom and for their fruit; and those like the vine, whose blossoms are of small account, and which men prize only for their fruit. Evidently God places here a high valuation on the last of these.

How tempted we are to display what is impressive to men, a blossom to be admired! But the Father has set us as branches in the Vine. There, what He seeks above all is fruit-bearing.

JUNE 3rd

Every branch that beareth fruit, he cleanseth it, that it may bear more fruit. John 15. 2.

Training of all kinds today is aimed at developing the soul of the natural man, to make him independent, proud, quick-witted, self-assured. This generation loves men that can get the better of others. In thus fitting them to Satan's use it is doing his work for him.

What God is engaged upon with you and me is the pruning work of the vinedresser. That untimely growth in our souls has to be checked and dealt with. God must cut it off. On the one hand He is seeking to bring us to the place where we live by the life of His Son, planted within us by new birth. On the other, He is doing a direct work in our hearts to weaken the fund of our natural resources which led in the first place to Adam's sin. Every day we are learning these two lessons: a rising up of the life of this One, and a checking and handing over to death of that other natural life, so that in the world's eyes we stand as weak, ignorant men who often have to admit: "I do not know—but He knows, and that is enough." May God deliver us from today's arrogance of soul!

JUNE 4th

When I am weak, then am I strong. 2 Corinthians 12. 10.

This paradox lies at the heart of true Christian experience. I came to see this in the course of a personal trial of my own, in which, like Paul with his thorn in the flesh, I had received the answer "No" to my prayer for relief. The thought came to me then of a river-boat that could not pass a deep narrows because of a boulder in the stream, jutting five feet or so up from the river bed. In my trial I had been asking the Lord to remove the boulder. Now within me the question arose: Would it be better to have the five-foot boulder out of the way, or to let Him raise the level of the water by five feet? To Paul's appeal the answer had been "My grace is sufficient." Of course it would be better to have the water-level raised! My problem was gone. For Christianity is not a matter of removing boulders, but of having deeper water!

JUNE 5th

As many as touched him were made whole. Mark 6. 56.

Recall the incident of the Pharisee and the publican at prayer in the temple. The Pharisee understood all about tithes and offerings, yet from him there was no cry of the heart to God. It was the publican who cried, "Lord have mercy upon me!" Something went out to God from that man which met with an immediate response, and Jesus singles him out as the one whom God reckoned righteous. For what is it to be reckoned righteous? It is to touch God. The great weakness of so much present preaching of the Gospel is that we try to make people understand the plan of salvation, and all too often we see little or no result. Wherein have we failed? I am sure it is in this, that our hearers do not see Him. We have not adequately presented the Person. We point them only to their sin or God's salvation, whereas their real need is to see the Saviour Himself, to meet Him and to make contact with Him.

JUNE 6th

Yea, all of you, gird yourself with humility, to serve one another. 1 Peter 5. 5.

The Body builds up itself in love. It is not that there are special apostolic workers who can stand apart from the Body as though it were a "thing", and build it up from the outside. There is a danger, to which we are all prone, of thinking of the Church of Christ as something outside of ourselves to which we are ministering. This is not possible. If we are to contribute to the life of the Body we must humbly take our place of submission within it, receiving from, as well as contributing to, its mutual ministry of life. Do we find it easier to humble our-selves towards God than towards our fellow believers? Re-member, without a continual exercise of humility, it is quite impossible to serve one another. For better or worse we are members of that Body, from which we cannot resign. Offend men and we offend God. Accept help from our brethren, and it is only that we may help others. Serve, and we ourselves are ministered to. We are God's fellow-workers, God's building.

JUNE 7th

Thus saith the Lord, the God of Israel, The barrel of meal shall not waste, neither shall the cruse of oil fail. 1 Kings 17. 14.

We are God's representatives in this world, set here to prove and to display His faithfulness. Our attitude, our words and our actions must all declare that He alone is our Source of supply. It is imperative, therefore, and supremely so in financial matters, that we be in a true sense independent of men and wholly cast upon God. If there is any weakness here, He will be robbed of the glory that is His due. As God's ser-vants we must show forth the abundance of His resources. We must not be afraid to *appear* wealthy before people. I do not suggest we should ever be untrue, but such an attitude is perfectly consistent with honesty. Let us keep our financial needs secret, even if our secrecy should lead men to conclude that we are well off when in fact we have nothing at all. He who sees in secret will take note of our needs, and He will meet them in no stinted measure but "according to His riches in glory by Christ Jesus". We dare to make things difficult for God, because He requires no assistance from us to perform His miracles.

JUNE 8th

Deep calleth unto deep. Psalm 42. 7.

Only deep can answer deep. Nothing that is merely of the shallows can respond to the depths, and only what goes deep in us can meet the deep needs of others. If we want to help those who are passing through floods, we must have been through floods ourselves. Have we a history of God's secret dealings, or does what men see represent all we have got? Many of us are shallow. We only seem to grow outwardly, with nothing in reserve. If we choose to live on the surface of things, we may be of some help to folk in need, but the happiness we bring them will pass. We shall not have been able really to meet them where they are. Paul had a secret he kept for fourteen long years, and what help has its eventual disclosure brought! When we have found God speaking to us in the depths, then it is we possess treasures of darkness to share with others in their hour of trial.

JUNE 9th

His eyes were as a flame of fire; and his feet like unto burnished brass . . . and his voice as the voice of many waters. Revelation 1. 14 f.

In the Book of Revelation God shows us an aspect of His Son not shown to us in the Gospels. In the Gospels we see Him as Saviour, in the Revelation as King. The one displays His love, the other His majesty. In the upper room Jesus girds Himself about the waist, for service; at Patmos He is discovered girt about the breasts, for war. In the Gospels His mild eyes melt Peter; in Revelation they are as a flame of fire. There His voice is gentle, calling His own sheep by name, and gracious words proceed out of His mouth; here His voice is terrible as the sound of many waters, and from His mouth a sharp two-edged sword strikes death to His foes. It is not enough that we know Jesus as Lamb of God and Saviour of the world; we must know Him also as God's King, God's Judge. When we see Him as Saviour, we exclaim "How lovable!" and lean on His bosom. When we see Him as Monarch, we cry "How terrible!" and fall prostrate at His feet.

JUNE 10th

God . . . made us to sit with him in the heavenly places, in Christ Jesus. Ephesians 2. 6.

What does it really mean to sit down? When we walk or stand we bear on our legs all the weight of our own body, whereas when we sit down our entire weight rests upon the chair or bench on which we sit. We grow weary when we walk or stand, but we feel rested when we have sat down for a while. In walking or standing we expend a great deal of energy, but when we are seated we relax at once, because the strain no longer falls upon our muscles and sinews but upon something outside ourselves. So too in spiritual things, to sit down is simply to rest our whole weight—our load, ourselves, our future, everything—upon the Lord. We let Him bear the responsibility, and cease to carry it ourselves.

JUNE 11th

As they ministered to the Lord and fasted, the Holy Ghost said, Separate me Barnabas and Saul for the work whereunto I have called them. Acts 13. 2.

No one can truly work for the Lord who has not first learned to minister to Him. It was while Barnabas and Saul ministered to the Lord and fasted that the voice of the Spirit was heard calling them to special service.

And it was to the divine call they responded, not to the appeal of human need. They had heard no reports of cannibals or head-hunting savages; their compassions had not been stirred by doleful tales of child-marriage, foot-binding or opium-smoking. They had heard no voice but the voice of the Spirit; they had seen no claims but the claims of Christ. It was the Lordship of Christ which claimed their service, and it was on His authority alone that they went forth.

JUNE 12th

We have no more than five loaves and two fishes; except we should go and buy food for all this people. Luke 9. 13.

When Jesus said "Give ye them to eat", it was not because He expected His disciples to have a plan, but because He wanted *them* to expect a miracle. Like us however they chose the easier way, the way which does not require the exercise of faith or prayer. Their solution was to "go and buy". It was a proposal unworthy of disciples; it could as well have been made by Pharisees or even Sadducees. It displayed no faith, no trust in Him. As John's Gospel makes plain, their thoughts were on their pockets. They had not enough money!

We only see what *we* can do. We shut our eyes to God and His inexhaustible resources. But God is not to be measured by us. Never mind what we can or cannot do; He is waiting to show us His miracles.

JUNE 13th

I have been crucified with Christ. Galatians 2. 20.

What does it mean for me to be "crucified"? I think the answer is best summed up in the words the crowd used of Jesus: "Away with him!" God never allows this matter of being crucified with Christ to remain for us a mere theory, though I confess that for many years it *was* no more than that to me. I myself had preached the Cross in these very terms without knowing it in my own experience—until one day I saw with dramatic suddenness that it had been I, Nee To-sheng, who died there with my Lord. "Away with him!" they had cried, and in saying it of Him they had also, unwittingly, echoed God's verdict upon me. And that sentence of God upon me was carried out in Him. This new discovery affected me almost as greatly as did my first discovery of salvation. I tell you, it left me so humbled as to be for a while quite unable to preach at all, whereas till that day, I have to admit, preaching had been my consuming passion.

JUNE 14th

Consecrate yourselves today to the Lord . . . that he
may bestow upon you a blessing. Exodus 32. 29.

Presenting myself to God "as alive from the dead"
(to use Paul's words) implies a recognition that henceforth I
am altogether His. This giving of myself is a definite act, just
as definite as believing in Jesus Christ. There must be a day in
my life when I pass out of my own hands into His, and from
that day forward I belong to Him and no longer to myself.
That does not mean that I consecrate myself to be a preacher
or a missionary. Alas, many people are missionaries merely
because they have consecrated their own natural gifts to His
work. But that is not true consecration. Then to what are we
to be consecrated? Not to "Christian work", but to *the will of*
God, to be and do whatever He requires.

JUNE 15th

For where two or three are gathered together in my name,
there am I in the midst of them. Matthew 18. 20.

The preceding verse has given a wonderful promise
of answered prayer, but the promise is conditional. There must
be at least two, and they in agreement. Why is their prayer
answered? Because these two or three "are gathered together
in my name". That is, they do not just meet; they are gathered
(passive voice). We see the difference, for to be gathered is not
merely to go of ourselves; it is to be moved by the Spirit of
God. And they come, not on their own affairs, but having a
single common concern for His. It is this that unites them in
His name. And when this is so, Jesus says, "I am in the midst

of them", leading, revealing, enlightening. Praise God, that is not a promise; it is a statement of fact!

JUNE 16th

The true worshippers shall worship the Father in spirit and truth: for such doth the Father seek to be his worshippers. John 4. 23.

The decalogue opens with God's claim to exclusive worship. This expression of God's will is not only His command, it is also His desire. But if the ten commandments show us what gives God joy, the temptations in the wilderness reveal what will bring joy to Satan. In both cases it is worship. So we have one thing that both God and Satan want. By it we can satisfy either heaven or hell. Worship is priceless. Satan's whole idea is to rob God of it by ensnaring His people into some kind of idolatry. Idolatry claims another, besides God, to be worthy of worship. It is our privilege to counter this by holding it exclusively for God.

JUNE 17th

This is life eternal, that they should know thee the only true God, and him whom thou didst send, even Jesus Christ. John 17. 3.

Men rejected Christ, not on the ground of what He did but of who He was, and they are invited to believe in what He is and who He is, and not, first of all, in what He has done. "He who hath the Son hath the life." The appreciation of His work must come, but the main question is whether or not you have the Son, and not, first of all, whether or not you understand the whole plan of salvation. The first condition of salvation is not knowledge, but meeting Christ.

There are people who you may feel were saved by the wrong scriptures! They were spoken to through verses that do not seem to point the way of salvation, and you almost feel they could not be saved on that basis! I used to wish that those whom I led to the Lord would be saved on the basis of a verse like John 3. 16, but I have come to see that all that is needed for the initial step is that there should be a personal touch with God. It does not matter, therefore, which scripture God elects to use for that first vital step.

JUNE 18th

One died for all, therefore all died. 2 Corinthians 5. 14.

Why does God say we are to reckon ourselves dead? Because we *are* dead. Suppose I have two dollars in my pocket, what do I enter in my account-book? Can I enter one dollar ninety-five cents or two dollars five? No, I must enter in my book what is in fact in my pocket, no more, no less. Accounting is the reckoning of facts, not fancies. God could not ask me to put down in my account-book what was not true. He could not ask me to reckon that I am dead if I am still alive. For such mental gymnastics the word "reckoning" would be quite inappropriate.

God asks us to do the account; to put down "I have died", and then to abide by it. Why? Because it is a fact. When the Lord Jesus was on the Cross, I was there in Him. Therefore I count it to be true. I count myself dead unto sin, but alive unto God in Christ Jesus.

JUNE 19th

I was in the Spirit on the Lord's day. Revelation 1. 10.

Who is qualified to study the Apocalypse? We find the answer in John's own history. His first vision was not of events but of Jesus Christ Himself. John, who had lain on Jesus' bosom, must have a sight of his eternal Lord that shattered him to the dust. Only then might he be shown "things to come". No one is qualified to study what follows who has not first seen what John saw; for not till we see Jesus thus are we equipped for conflict.

Before this John knew the love of the Lord, now he beheld His majesty. Then he knew Him as compassionate Saviour, now as glorious King. Unless we have first seen Him thus and have fallen as dead at His feet, a knowledge of coming events will only stimulate our curiosity and puff us up, producing eventual confusion or even disbelief. This book proclaims the battle of the Lord. It declares war on all that defies His kingdom. Its aim therefore is to show us Christ Jesus as King on the Throne. Only such a sight creates warriors.

JUNE 20th

There will I meet with thee, and I will commune with thee from above the mercy seat, from between the two cherubim which are upon the ark of the testimony. Exodus 25. 22.

What is the basis of our communion with God? It is His glory. At the mercy-seat with its shadowing cherubim we have fellowship with God, and they are "cherubim of glory".

It is in the place where God's glory is manifested, with its implied judgment upon man, that we find mercy—there and there alone. Cannot God, being God, show mercy where He will? No, He can only show mercy where His moral glory is also maintained. He does not divorce the mercy-seat from the cherubim.

It is the shed blood that makes communion possible for sinful man. Because of it God can show mercy without violating His glory; He can commune with man without denying Himself. Thus the blood of Christ is essential to fellowship, absolutely essential. Nevertheless it is not the basis of fellowship. When I commune with God at His mercy-seat it is not on the precious blood I gaze, but on the glory. The veil is taken away, and with unveiled face we all behold the glory of God.

JUNE 21st

Brother Saul, the Lord, even Jesus, who appeared unto thee in the way which thou camest, hath sent me. Acts 9. 17.

How often can we get help from those whom we might naturally despise! When the blinded Saul reached Damascus all he knew was that some God-sent messenger would tell him what to do. At first no man came. Only after three days of darkness did someone at length arrive, and even then he was but "a disciple". From Luke's use of this simple title we are to conclude that though devout and honourable, Ananias was just an ordinary brother, with nothing special to qualify him as helper of the destined great apostle of the Church.

And for his part too, Ananias, who knew Saul of Tarsus by repute and had every reason to fear him, must now give practical expression to a miracle of divine grace in his own heart. By his simple words of greeting he expressed his recognition of another member of Christ. So in one Spirit the two men, brethren now, gave and received counsel that was destined by God to have world-shaking repercussions.

JUNE 22nd

If any man buildeth on the foundation gold, silver, costly stones, wood, hay, stubble; each man's work shall be made manifest: for the day shall declare it, because it is revealed in fire. 1 Corinthians 3. 12 f.

It is weight that counts. Wood, hay, stubble are cheap, light, perishable. Gold, silver, precious stones are costly, weighty, eternal. Here is the key to Paul's meaning. God looks not only at the work done but at the material used, and readily distinguishes the solid from the superficial worker. The heavy metals, the gold of the divine character and glory, the silver of His redemptive work: these are the materials He prizes. Not merely what we preach, but what we are, weighs with God: not "Where is the need most evident? What ideas and resources have I got? How much can I do?" but "Where is God moving? What is there of Christ there? What is the mind of the Spirit in this?" When our work has that character we can be sure it will survive.

JUNE 23rd

I will give thee thanks for ever, because thou hast done it:
and I will wait on thy name, for it is good. Psalm 52. 9.

The test of time is the hardest test of all. Yet only by learning to wait for God do we find ourselves involved in something really done by Him. Ten years after he had believed God for a son, Abram felt he could wait no longer. He knew God intended him to have an heir so he sought to provide one, and Ishmael was the result. It was not Abram's motive that was wrong, but his starting point. He felt he could still do something to produce a child, as indeed he could, and did. At eighty-six he yet had that capacity.

There followed a further long wait, until at the age of a hundred Abraham could no longer do even this; his body was "as good as dead" (Romans 4. 19). It was to such a man, powerless now in himself to please God, that the marvellous gift of grace came in the person of Isaac. This was wholly God's doing and well worth waiting for. To have God do His own work through us, even once, is better than a lifetime of human striving.

JUNE 24th

So mightily grew the word of the Lord and prevailed.
Acts 19. 20.

As the apostles worked, the blessing of the Lord rested on their labours. We shall do well if we follow in their steps, but we must understand clearly that simply to adopt apostolic methods is not enough. Unless we have apostolic consecration, apostolic faith and apostolic power, we shall still fail to see apostolic results. I do not suggest we should under-estimate the value of their methods; they are essential if we are to see equivalent results. But we must not overlook the even greater need of apostolic spirituality, nor be dismayed if along the way we encounter apostolic trials.

JUNE 25th

Know ye not that ye are a temple of God, and that the Spirit of God dwelleth in you? 1 Corinthians 3. 16.

A revelation of the indwelling Spirit was the remedy Paul offered the Corinthian Christians for their unholiness. Their need, like ours today, was to grasp the fact that God Himself had taken up His abode in them. To many of us the Holy Spirit of God is quite unreal. We regard Him as a mere influence—an influence for good, no doubt, but no more than that. In our thinking, conscience and the Spirit are more or less identified as some "thing" within us that brings us to book when we are bad and tries to show us how to be good. Like the Corinthians our trouble is not that we lack God's gift of the indwelling Spirit, but that we have not yet awakened to the reality of His presence. We fail to appreciate the essential holiness of the One who has made His abode within our hearts.

The Spirit said unto Philip, Go near, and join thyself to this chariot. Acts 8. 29.

Divine work must be divinely initiated. A worker may be called directly by the Spirit, or indirectly through the reading of the Word, through preaching, or through circumstances; but whatever the means God uses to make known His will to a man, *His* must be the Voice heard through every other voice. *He* must be the One who speaks, no matter through what instrument the call may come. Of course it is wrong to reject out of hand the opinion of fellow-workers, but it is also wrong to accept their opinions as a substitute for the direct witness of His Spirit. While it is true we must never be independent of the other members of the Body, let us never forget also that it is from the Head that all our direction comes.

The Lord of hosts is with us; the God of Jacob is our refuge. Psalm 46. 11.

How like our own is Jacob's history! Until God begins to deal with us, we are inclined to take a superior attitude to Jacob's intrigues, but as we begin to encounter the deviousness of our own thinking, we soon recognize the man's essential character in ourselves. And remember, what changed Jacob's life from vanity to profit was nothing less than the power of divine grace.

Ishmael might talk of the God of Abraham, Esau could

perhaps claim to have some dealings with the God of Abraham and of Isaac, but both of them, in doing so, could only look back. Theirs was no personal experience of Him. We read nothing of the God of Ishmael or of Esau. But for Jacob, and for us too, this is not enough. Our God is a present refuge, a present power. Like Moses at the burning bush we must hear Him say: "I am the God of Abraham, the God of Isaac, and the God of Jacob." In such a God there is hope for us all.

JUNE 28th

Having been buried with him in baptism, wherein ye were also raised with him through faith in the working of God.
Colossians 2. 12.

Alas, some have been taught to look on burial as a means to death; they try to die by getting themselves buried! Let me say emphatically that unless our eyes have been opened by God to see that we have died in Christ and been buried with Him, we have no right to be baptized. The reason we step down into the water is that we recognize that in God's sight we have already died. It is to this that we testify. God's question is clear and simple. "Christ has died, and I have included you there. Now, what are you going to say to that?" What is my answer? "Lord, I believe you have done the crucifying. I say Yes to the death and to the burial to which You have committed me." He has consigned me to death and the grave; by my request for baptism I give public assent to that fact.

JUNE 29th

He that dwelleth in the secret place of the Most High shall abide under the shadow of the Almighty. Psalm 91. 1.

The object of temptation is always to get us to do something. During the early months of the Japanese war in China we lost a great many tanks, and so were unable to deal with the Japanese armour, until the following scheme was devised. A single shot would be fired at a Japanese tank by one of our snipers in ambush. After a considerable lapse of time the first shot would be followed by a second; then, after a further silence, by another shot; until the tank driver, eager to locate the source of the annoyance, would pop his head out to look around. The next shot, carefully aimed, would put an end to him. As long as he remained under cover he was perfectly safe. The whole scheme was devised to bring him out into the open. In the same way, Satan's temptations are designed to entice us to expose ourselves. He knows well that as soon as we step out of our Hiding Place, as soon as we move from the cover of Christ and act in self-dependence, he has scored a victory.

JUNE 30th

The flesh lusteth against the Spirit, and the Spirit against the flesh: for these are contrary the one to the other; that ye may not do the things that ye would. Galatians 5. 17.

Consider carefully what this says. "The flesh" in us is not opposed to us but to the Holy Spirit of God. It is He, not we, who meets and deals with its promptings. And with what result? "That ye may not do the things that ye would." I think we have often failed to grasp the import of that last clause. What "would we do" naturally? We would disregard the divine will and move off on some course of action dictated by our own instincts. The effect, therefore, of our refusal to come out of the cover of Christ and act of ourselves is that the Holy Spirit is free to do *His* work—free, that is, to meet and deal with the flesh in us, so that in fact we shall *not* do what we naturally would do. Instead of going off on a plan and course of our own, we shall find our joy in His perfect plan.

JULY 1st

Giving diligence to keep the unity of the Spirit in the bond of peace. There is one body, and one Spirit, even as also ye were called in one hope of your calling. Ephesians 4. 3 f.

There are several elements in that unity of the Spirit which is our common heritage. One of them is our hope. This is not just a cheerful optimism; it is the hope of our calling as Christians. What is our hope as Christians? It is to be with the Lord for ever in glory. There is not a single soul who is truly His in whose heart there is not this hope, for to have Christ in us is to have in us "the hope of glory". If anyone claims to be the Lord's and has no expectation of heaven or of glory, his is an empty profession. Furthermore, all who share this hope are one, for since we have the hope of being together for all eternity, how can we be divided in time? If we are going to share the same future, shall we not gladly share the same present?

JULY 2nd

A certain Samaritan, as he journeyed, came where he was: and when he saw him, he was moved with compassion, and came to him. Luke 10. 33 f.

What the helpless sinner cannot do, the Saviour is at hand to do for him. The Lord Jesus came as a Friend of sinners, to help sinners approach Him. Our coming to Him was made possible by His first coming to us. By it heaven was brought within our reach. I remember I was once sitting talking to a brother in his home. His wife and mother were upstairs, but his small son was in the sitting-room with us. Presently the little fellow wanted something, and called out to his mother for it. "It is up here," she replied. "Come up and get it." But he cried out to her, "I can't, Mummy; it's such a long way. Please bring it down to me." And indeed he was very small and the stairs were steep; so down she came with it. And salvation is just like that. Only by His coming to us could our need be met. Had He not come, we sinners could never have approached Him; but He "came down from heaven", and we are lifted up.

JULY 3rd

The Lord hath taken you, and brought you forth out of the iron furnace, out of Egypt, to be unto him a people of inheritance. Deuteronomy 4. 20.

Nowhere in either Old or New Testament is dedication divorced from redemption. The two are intimately linked and we never find the one without the other. The

Apostle Paul did not wait until he was a prisoner or about to be martyred before presenting himself to God. That had taken place at his conversion on the road to Damascus. Never was it God's plan that His people should wait several years, perhaps for a time of special blessing, before giving themselves wholly to Him. In His intention, when He saves a people He also gains a people. He gives me redemption; He asks for my self-dedication in return. Because of His wonderful gift to me, I give myself to God.

JULY 4th

God loveth a cheerful giver. 2 Corinthians 9. 7.

The servant of the Lord should learn to give as well as to receive. Yet how hard it often is to do so! I remember once I was setting out on a journey up river to take part in some important meetings. I had to trust the Lord for my fare, and I had only eighteen dollars in hand. The river boat would take me only so far, and I might need anything up to $300 to hire a boat for the rest of the way. Yet before I left, God told me to give away to a friend six of my sorely needed dollars. I started off, found quite unforeseen cheap travel provided from half way, enjoyed a most blessed week, and was amply provided for for my return journey. What a joy to discover when I got back that my gift of six dollars had been desperately needed!

All too often, I fear, we are bad givers. If I am only a receiver and not also a giver, I am unworthy of the God who sent me. The divine principle is not "Save and you shall grow rich." It is "Give and it shall be given unto you."

JULY 5th

Jesus therefore took the loaves. John 6. 11.

For most of His miracles God makes use of material. Here Jesus accepts five loaves and two fishes. He might have turned stones to bread, but He did not. He chose instead to work with what was offered Him. "Bring them hither to me," he said. What He does, He does through us. All miracles begin here, with my all in His hands. Keep my loaves to myself, and one man is fed. Give them up to Him, and shall I go hungry?

In a day of extreme national poverty the prophet Malachi brought to Israel God's answer to her problem. It was: Bring the whole tithe into the storehouse—and see! It takes only a tiny stopper to close a very large bottle, so withholding from us its entire contents. And heaven is like that. Often for us there is no miracle, simply because we give God nothing to work on. He asks only a very little—what we have! But He needs that.

JULY 6th

What are these among so many? John 6. 9.

The hopes of too many are still centred, not on the Lord's blessing but on the state of their treasury, the few paltry loaves in their own hands. What we have in hand is so pitifully little, and yet we keep reckoning with it; and the more we reckon the darker the prospect. My friends, miracles issue from the blessing of the Lord! Where that rests, thousands are fed; where it is lacking much more than two hundred pennyworth will never suffice. Recognize that fact, and we shall see a transformation in our work. There will be no more need to manipulate, no more need to dodge; there will be no call for human contriving nor for large, empty speeches, for we shall simply trust God and await His miracle. And where we have already made a mess of things, even there we may find that somehow all is well. A little bit of blessing can carry us over a great deal of trouble.

JULY 7th

It shall come to pass that the man whom I shall choose, his rod shall bud. Numbers 17. 5.

Aaron's priesthood had been contested. People were questioning whether he was indeed God's chosen. "Is this man ordained of God or not?" they asked. "We do not really know!" God set out therefore to prove who was His servant and who was not. How did He do so? Twelve rods were placed before Him in the sanctuary, and were left there for a night. In the morning His choice was seen in the rod which budded, blossomed and bore fruit.

New buds, flowers, ripe almonds: all these proclaim the miracle of resurrection. It is life out of death that marks divinely attested ministry—that, and that alone. Without it you have nothing. God can only use as His ministers those who, through union with Him, have come to taste the power of an endless life.

JULY 8th

*He that is entered into his rest hath himself also rested from
his works, as God did from his.* Hebrews 4. 10.

At his creation man stood in a highly significant
relation to God's rest. Adam, we are told, was created on the
sixth day. Clearly then, he had no part in God's first six days
of work, for only at their end did he exist. Thus God's
seventh day was Adam's first. Whereas God worked six days
to enjoy His sabbath rest, Adam began life with the sabbath.
God works before He rests. Man, to be in harmony with God,
must first enter into God's rest; then alone can he work. This
principle underlies all Christian service. Moreover, it was
because God's first creation was so truly complete that Adam's
life could have this satisfying starting-point. And here is the
Gospel: that for us sinners God has taken one further necessary
step, and has completed also the entire work of salvation. We
need do nothing whatsoever to merit it. At once, by an act of
simple faith, we can enter into the sabbath rest of His finished
work.

JULY 9th

*The accuser of our brethren is cast down, which accuseth
them before our God day and night.* Revelation 12. 10.

Satan is a murderer and a deceiver, he entices and he
attacks; but today he specializes in accusing. Heaven re-
cognizes this, and so must every Christian. Night and day he
accuses us, and his charges, which are not unfounded, are
directed at our conscience—the very point where we most
lack the strength to fight him. His object is to drive us to think

in despair, "I am a hopeless failure! God can do nothing with me!" Conscience is a precious thing, but to repeat endlessly "I am no good! I am no good!" is not Christian humility. To confess our sins is wholesome, but let us never carry confession to the point where our sinfulness looms for us larger than the work of Christ. The Devil knows no weapon more effective against you and me than the creation of this illusion. What is the remedy? Plead guilty *to God*. Confess to Him "Lord, I am no good!" but then remind yourself of the precious Blood, and looking away to His glory, add: "But Lord, I am abiding in Thee!"

JULY 10th

Be still, and know that I am God; I will be exalted. Psalm 46. 10.

If God's throne seems to rock, can our hand steady it? Some appear to think so. One such was Jacob. God had clearly stated that he should rule, and in all he did he aimed only to forward God's plans. He saw God's election and he embraced it—but then one day he learned that his father had sent Esau hunting with a view to giving him the blessing. If that happened, where was God's promise?

Something must be done! The clever, capable man was also a schemer, so he set out to do for God what it looked as though God could not do for Himself—and to achieve it he cheated his father. But of he seemed to gain from his cheating had to be abandoned, and he was forced to flee. Yes, he was God's choice, God wanted him, but as yet he knew neither his God nor himself. What in fact he received was a severe dose of the divine discipline. Clever people get a lot of that!

JULY 11th

Whatsoever a man soweth, that shall he also reap. Galatians 6. 7.

God's practical dealings with us His children follow principles peculiarly His own which faithfully express His ways. Are our sins forgiven in Christ? Then it is our privilege henceforth, to be gently handled in ways designed always to warn us when, for a moment, our course is not His. Often this means that what we are going through today is directly connected with something in our past, a reaping of what we have earlier sown. Have we been gracious? Then grace is multiplied to us. Were we critical of someone's action? Then sooner or later we discover ourselves doing that very thing—and reaping the consequences. For with what measure we mete it is meted to us again, *by God.* "If you knew what was wrong with your brother you should have known what was wrong with you!" That is the principle. His way is not harsh, for it is a way of love, so measured as to offer us all possible safeguards. Welcome it, and we shall escape many an unseen hazard.

JULY 12th

With what measure ye mete it shall be measured to you again. Luke 6. 38.

I knew a dear brother who was intensely critical. His favourite observation was: "It is the hand of God." Was someone sick? "It is the hand of God on him," he would say. Sometimes maybe he was right. But one day another brother, of whom he disapproved, lost his son, and, believe it or not, received a letter from this man saying, "It is the hand of God on you"! I saw the letter and felt highly indignant that he should thus judge another. What was my horror, then, when within two weeks his own son was taken ill and died. Then it was that temptation came to me. I took up my pen and wrote, "My dear brother, I grieve with you in your bereavement, but if that man lost his child because the hand of God was on him in judgment, then what about yourself? Are you willing to admit that God's hand is on you?" It seemed about time this was said! I finished the letter—and then God rebuked me. Was not I doing the very thing I had disapproved of? His mercy had restrained me just in time. I tore up the letter. If I too would not reap, I must not sow!

JULY 13th

We are his workmanship, created in Christ Jesus for good works, which God afore prepared that we should walk in them. Ephesians 2. 10.

The first clause could as well be rendered, "We are his masterpiece." The Church is the very best God can produce. It can never be improved on. We look around and see breakdown everywhere, and we wonder, "What is the Church coming to?" I tell you, she is not "coming to" anything; she has arrived. We do not look forward to discover her goal; we look back. God reached His end in Christ before the foundation of the world. As we move on with Him in the light of that eternal fact, we witness even now its progressive manifestation. In Romans 8. 30 Paul tells us that those God has foreordained He has both called and justified and glorified. Thus all His own have, in His intention, already been glorified. In Christ the goal is reached. The Church has already come to glory!

JULY 14th

Thou art the Christ, the Son of the living God. Matthew
16. 16.

Death is the power, the weapon, of the gates of hell.
This is still true today; yet until God has opened our eyes to
see it, we shall scarcely know the value of speaking out in confession of Him. But when suddenly, in some till now unfore-
seen circumstance, we find to our dismay that apparently faith
does not work, prayer does not work, our very spirits are
paralysed—then it is we shall learn the need to proclaim
Christ. In so doing we shall discover what it was God was
waiting for. "Thou art Lord. Thou art Victor. Thou art
King." The best prayer of all is not "I want" but "Thou art".
By the revelation given to us, let us speak. In prayer meetings,
at the Lord's Table, alone before the Lord, in the midst of the
thronging world, or in the dark hour of need, learn to proclaim "Thou art!"

JULY 15th

*When Abram heard that his brother was taken captive, he
led forth his trained men . . . and pursued.* Genesis
14. 14.

Lot had been quick to settle down in the land; before
long he was to lose his possessions in it. By contrast, as this
chapter reminds us, Abram was the Hebrew, the "passer-
over", the pilgrim. It is they who are content to remain in
transit in the land of promise who have real power against its
foes.

Abram had been right to leave the matter of possessions

with God, but he would have been quite wrong at the same time to have dismissed Lot from his love and concern. In this he was a true overcomer: before going out to pursue the kings he had won the victory in his own spirit. How easy to have nursed a grievance against his self-seeking kinsman! At the very least his attitude to the calamity might justly have been "I told you so!" But no, a grievance is no basis for victory. In all such circumstances we too must first win the battle in our own hearts. Is the man my brother? Then however he may have wronged or injured me, for the Lord's sake I must love him, pray for him, mobilize my forces to his aid.

JULY 16th

For of him, and through him, and unto him, are all things.
To him be the glory for ever. Romans 11. 36.

God must be the Originator of all spiritual work. His will must govern its beginnings; on this we are all agreed. Indeed we would go further and say that all is to end too with Him, so that, in Paul's words, "God may be all in all." But there is something more. He is not only the Originator and the Consummator of all things; He is the Worker too. And where His power is at work, all will issue in glory. Our trouble is that, while we know the beginning must be "of Him" and the end "unto Him", we forget the other vital fact, that all in the middle, all the great activity that lies between, must be "through Him". If He is to have glory at the last, we must be in no position to claim any. God's will governs the beginning, His glory the end, but His power must permeate the whole operation between. In practice the question of glory is settled, not at the end, but in the middle.

JULY 17th

Grow in the grace and knowledge of our Lord and Saviour
Jesus Christ. 2 Peter 3. 18.

We long to see men saved from perishing and won
for God's glory. But, do we stop there? When we see three or
four thousand converts—or even three or four !—all saved and
all going on fairly well with the Lord, do we feel a task has
been accomplished? Should we not regard it rather as a task
just begun? Ought we not to ask ourselves how many of them
have yet caught a glimpse of the one heavenly Man into which
God has brought them? Are they still just units, fishes in the
net, figures in a list of "campaign results", or does that supreme vision possess them? It will certainly not do so unless it
first possesses us. So I ask again, are we burdened, as were the
apostles, to see them grow up in all things into the Head, even
Christ?

JULY 18th

Not one of them shall fall on the ground without your
Father. Matthew 10. 29.

God is a God of purpose. Creation was no accident,
but the expression of a definite purpose on the part of God. A
great passage in Ephesians 1 speaks of His choice of us
"according to the good pleasure of his will", and tells us that
according to His purpose "we should be to the praise of his
glory, we who before hoped in Christ". When we think of
Adam's fall, and of our own sin, and of the meagreness of our

response to Him who by the grace of God tasted death for every man, we are wholly amazed at this. Can these things be? we ask ourselves. It is well, then, to be reminded that even the death of a sparrow, too trifling for us to note, is a thing of which God takes account. The Creator of the whole universe has a will regarding even one sparrow. "Fear not therefore; ye are of more value than many sparrows."

JULY 19th

My God shall fulfil every need of yours according to his riches in glory in Christ Jesus. Philippians 4. 19.

Many Christians are so poor they have not even sufficient to meet their own needs. Alas for any who go to them for help! Others are so rich you can never assess their wealth. You never seem to meet a difficulty they have not met, nor find yourself in a situation where they are unable to help. They seem to have resources enough for all who come to them in need. Many Christians do not go utterly bankrupt simply because they are being ministered to by others, who continually pour their own spiritual wealth into the Body. Such folk little know their debt to other believers, some of whom they might even be tempted to despise. It may be, when a friend comes from a journey and expects bread from us, that the Lord will permit us to turn to a neighbour for something to give him. But what if He should say to us, "Give ye them to eat"?

JULY 20th

Whom have I in heaven but thee? And there is none upon earth that I desire beside thee. Psalm 73. 25.

Our complete surrender of ourselves to the Lord often hinges upon some particular thing, and God waits for that one thing. He must have it, for He must have our all. I was greatly impressed by something a great national leader wrote in his autobiography: "I want nothing for myself; I want everything for my country." If a man can be willing that his country should have everything and he himself nothing, cannot we say to our God: "Lord, I want nothing for myself; I want all for Thee. I will be what Thou willest, and I want to have nothing outside Thy will."? Not until we take the place of a servant can He take His place as Lord. He is not calling us to devote ourselves to His cause; He is asking us to yield ourselves unconditionally to His will.

JULY 21st

Ye are the light of the world. Matthew 5. 14.

Some ask, should they preach? or should they seek employment in a profession or trade? *Are* there two roads in front of a child of God? Where in Scripture do we find such alternatives: to preach *or* find work? Is it a choice we are called upon to make? God's people are a lamp for witness. Is there then a Christian who is *not* to witness? It cannot be that a few preach, while in some mysterious sense all are the lamp. No, there is a living witness for God on earth and for that I live. This is the one road for us all and there is no other. None can be the Lord's and not testify to Him. All must preach Christ; that is the big thing. It is a secondary question whether all the time is to be given to it or some spent in breadwinning. For everything turns on where our centre is. God cannot use one who adds preaching to business; He can use one who adds business to preaching. It simply depends which side the addition is on! God, not our business, is to be the centre of our lives.

JULY 22nd

All thy estimations shall be according to the shekel of the sanctuary. Leviticus 27. 25.

Numbers opens with a census of all in Israel of an age to go forth to war. Just before it, in this last chapter of Leviticus, God provides an assessment of His children's value in terms of their self-dedication to Him. (Distinguish this carefully from the passage in Exodus 30 where the redemption price, which is identical for every soul, represented what God Himself had done for them.) Here God has a definite estimate of each one, and a quick comparison of Leviticus 27. 3 with Numbers 1. 3 makes it clear that preciousness to Him is measured in terms of readiness for war. This raises for us the question: Are we available to take our part in the age-long battle of the Lord? Jehovah is a Man of war, and energy for war is what He prizes most highly. Old or young, whatever the length of our spiritual history, the question each must ask himself today is: What, in terms of battle-preparedness, is my value to God in the sanctuary?

JULY 23rd

Let thine eyes look right on, and let thine eyelids look straight before thee. Proverbs 4. 25.

For us who are God's children the most soul-destroying thing is to turn our gaze inward. Introspection is a deadly disease. Have we realized this? Sin we readily recognize as deadly, but introspection is less obviously suspect; and it is the unsuspected disease that is more to be feared than the apparent one. If I put to you the question: "Is it wrong to be proud?" you know the answer. If I ask again: "What about envy?" you reply: "Of course it is wrong!" Yet you can turn in on yourself a score of times in a single day, imagining that in doing so you are being particularly spiritual, and be totally unaware of the evil of it.

Stop doing it! Learn to walk in the Spirit. Do you feel moved to preach Christ to a soul? Do you stay and examine yourself whether this urge is from you or from God. While you are asking your questions, the opportunity will be gone! Act, and you will be liberated.

JULY 24th

Present yourself unto God, as alive from the dead, and your members as instruments of righteousness unto God. Romans 6. 13.

Many have taken this word "present" to imply con-secration, without looking carefully into its content. Of course that is what it does mean, but not in the sense in which we are inclined to understand it. It is not the consecration of our "old man" with his instincts and resources, his natural wisdom, strength and other gifts, to the Lord God for Him to use. This will be clear at once from the little clause "as alive from the dead". It defines for us the point at which consecration begins. For what is to be consecrated is not what belongs to the old creation, but only what has passed through death to resurrection. The "presenting" spoken of is the outcome of my knowing my old man to be crucified, and my reckoning myself alive unto God in Christ Jesus. Knowing, reckoning, presenting ourselves to Him: that is the divine order.

JULY 25th

And there we saw the Nephilim, the sons of Anak . . . and we were in our own sight as grasshoppers, and so we were in their sight. Numbers 13. 33.

Two thrones are at war. God claims the earth for His dominion. His arch-enemy, supported by spiritual hosts of wickedness, seeks instead to overrun it with evil, and thereby to exclude God from His own kingdom. We, God's people, are called upon to displace these mighty foes from their present realm and to make Christ head over all. What are we doing about it?

"If the Lord delight in us, then he will bring us into this land." This was the minority view of Joshua and Caleb in face of the ten spies' gloomy forecasts. *If the Lord delight in us.* One thing is certain: all talk of spiritual warfare remains but talk unless we have first learned to live a holy life. For the Nephilim *are* great, and we *are* grasshoppers; there is no disguising this. We realize it, and so do they! How do we live a life that is a delight to the Lord? Only by basing it on a true rest in Christ and in what He has done. If we lack this, Satan can afford to ignore us. With it, "their defence is removed from over them". We are more than conquerors *through Him*.

JULY 26th

So then death worketh in us, but life in you. 2 Corinthians
4. 12.

How precious is the Cross of Christ! It lies within
the scope of every single member to raise the tide of life in the
whole Body, provided only he will let the Cross deal drastic-
ally with the life of nature in him. You ask me how you can
be used to minister life to others. Not by setting out to do a lot
of things, nor yet by going into retirement and doing nothing
at all, but simply by letting the power of His death and resurrection operate in the course of your walk with God. Those
who serve only by words or works find their ministry brought
to a standstill if at any time circumstances reduce them to in-
activity or silence. To be used, they must be doing or speaking.
But this should not, and need not, be so. Only let "the dying
of Jesus" work in you, and life will surely manifest itself in
others. It must be so, for it is an abiding principle of the Body
that "death worketh in us but life in you".

JULY 27th

*Five of you shall chase an hundred, and an hundred of you
shall chase ten thousand: and your enemies shall fall before
you.* Leviticus 26.8.

Here surely is a picture of our prayer. For when we
agree on earth, heaven binds ten thousand foes. How often
have the people of God, in an hour of crisis, taken these words
of Jesus at their face value and proved them! So on the night
when Peter lay in prison, the church throughout Jerusalem got
to its knees and prayed earnestly, and all Herod's authority

was as nothing before the response of heaven to that prayer. Another Kingdom had invaded his territory, and even the great prison door yielded and gave way of itself.

JULY 28th

Quench not the Spirit. 1 Thessalonians 5. 19.

Every one of us should expect to receive from God some burden to be discharged through prayer. It is as we faithfully discharge it that He entrusts to us fresh ones. The only reason we do not receive more is that we have neglected to discharge those He has already given. Unload them in prayer, and we shall find His reward is to trust us with new and weightier responsibilities.

It is vital to be sensitive in our spirits to God, for it is all too possible, by quenching the Holy Spirit, to forfeit this ministry. Should we do so, the way of recovery is to confess to Him our sin, then to respond faithfully and instantly to each new Spirit-given impression. Has He laid someone on your heart? Send up an appeal to God for him at once. Oh, my friend, if you hope to serve God usefully, recover your lost burden! Be faithful in prayer. The instant you are moved to pray, pray!

JULY 29th

The hand of the Lord was strong upon me. Ezekiel 3. 4.

All true work for God springs from a prayer burden originating with the Holy Spirit's urge upon your spirit. Try working without such a burden, and what you do is likely to prove labour in vain. But work from the knowledge of a compulsion placed upon you by God Himself, and you will find your whole being is increasingly liberated as you go forward. Moreover work so performed is sure of spiritual value. So, if you are seeking to serve God effectively, wait on Him till He communicates to you His burden and thus makes known His will. Is it a burden to speak of Christ to someone? Give expression to it first in prayer, for the ministry of prayer is indispensable to God's service. Then go out and do it.

JULY 30th

As unknown, and yet well known; as dying, and behold we live; as chastened, and not killed; as sorrowful, yet alway rejoicing; as poor, yet making many rich; as having nothing, and yet possessing all things. 2 Corinthians 6. 9 f.

To be a Christian is to be a person in whom seeming incompatibles co-exist, but in whom it is the power of God that repeatedly triumphs. A Christian is one in whose life there is inherent a mysterious paradox, and this paradox is of God. How can power be manifested to perfection in a weak man? By Christianity; for Christianity *is* that very thing. It is not the removal of weakness, nor yet is it merely the manifestation of divine power. It is the manifestation of that power in the presence of human weakness. For what God is doing in us is neither merely negative nor merely positive. It is both together. He does not eliminate our infirmity, nor does He bestow His strength just anywhere at random. No, He leaves us with the infirmity, and He bestows His strength *there*.

JULY 31st

All the saints salute you, especially they that are of Caesar's household. Philippians 4. 22.

Have you ever come across the Church that Paul describes in Ephesians 1. 18 in terms of "the riches of the glory of his inheritance in the saints"? Or that depicted in I Corinthians 6. 11 as "washed . . . sanctified . . . justified in the name of the Lord Jesus, and in the Spirit of our God"? Oh, you say, that describes the position of the Church, but look at the condition of the churches! No, I reply, it describes the reality of the Church. In addressing the Romans Paul was more daring than were some of his translators. He wrote "called saints", or "saints by calling", but they felt it was running too great a risk to translate this literally, so they safeguarded their conception of spiritual things by writing "called *to be* saints". If we are only called "to be" saints, how long shall we have to be "being" before we can actually *be*? Praise God, we *are* saints!

AUGUST 1st

The city was pure gold, like unto pure glass. Revelation 21. 18.

Gold speaks to us of something wholly of God; glass, of what is transparently pure. Might we adapt the latter simile, and suggest that *future* purity is well illustrated by glass, *present* purity by water? For water can readily become clouded with defilement, but no impurity can enter the texture of glass. Our purity today is still liable to change; our purity then will never alter. The "divine nature" imparted to us is pure gold; there is no question of that. But, alas, we contribute to it a sorry admixture of dross, so that God's chief work in us is one of subtraction. By the Cross He is seeking to eliminate the mixture, bringing to the judgment of His death all in us that is of ourselves. For the most precious thing *we* have it in our power to produce—is dross. And that must go, all of it, ere we find our place amid the pure gold of God's eternal city.

AUGUST 2nd

Father, glorify thy name. John 12. 28.

We are given a great deal of Christ's teaching, but here is one of those rare, intimate occasions when He reveals Himself. A passage of doctrine ends with verse 26, and now the Son of man Himself shines out. "What shall I say? Father, save me from this hour?" He is off His guard, as it were, exposing what He really is, but He does not speak carelessly. When speaking to His Father, no less than when preaching to men, the Cross rules Him. "For this cause came I unto this hour." I cannot say "Save me". This is what I can say: "Father, glorify thy name!"

When the heart is troubled, speak carefully. The Lord did.

AUGUST 3rd

He shall sit as a refiner and purifier of silver, and shall purify the sons of Levi, and purge them as gold and silver. Malachi 3. 3.

What do we prize in a day when values are slipping: the dross of human cleverness and worldly resources, or the gold and silver of divine origin and redemption through

Christ? Many things in Christianity have become too cheap today, but there is no easy short-cut to spiritual worth. Preaching, prayer, witness, these may not seem difficult, but to be of value they will be costly in years and blood and divine discipline. God's "vessel unto honour" is the man who has waited for the Spirit to teach him, and who has not been ashamed meanwhile to admit he does not know. For there comes a day when the true character of things is tested. Preaching, in an hour of departure and confusion, is of little value unless men see God in it. At such a time they can tell whether the speaker has really been taken by God through the things of which he speaks. What has not already touched him deeply will have little power to touch others in that day.

AUGUST 4th

We will not serve thy gods, nor worship the golden image which thou hast set up. Daniel 3. 18.

The issue which governed Israel's rise or fall was the issue of true worship or idolatry. The revival under king Hezekiah was a revival of worship first of all. So was that under Zerubbabel. The Captivity was a severe punishment, but its severity for the Israelite lay above all in its termination of their worship. For when God does not receive His portion, His people lose theirs, and the greatest of all punishments is to be forbidden to serve God.

"Our God is a consuming fire." Whatever in us can be burned, will be. I am always moved when I see our Indian brethren fall on their faces in worship. "Reverence and awe" in the presence of God are seemly in us all. Where these exist and our hearts are right with Him, we His children cannot be burned. This was the experience of Daniel's three friends.

They were clear above all on the vital issue of worship. Our God *whom we serve* is able to deliver us, they said. What was Nebuchadnezzar's paltry furnace to men who did their obeisance before the everlasting burnings? They had nothing that could be consumed.

AUGUST 5th

These are written, that ye may believe that Jesus is the Christ, the Son of God; and that believing ye may have life in his name. John 20. 31.

I was once holding meetings in a college in South China. There I found an old schoolfellow of mine was now Professor of Psychology, so before the meetings began I went to call on him, and spoke to him of Christ. After listening a while politely, he said smiling, "It's no good preaching to me. I don't believe there is a God!"

Next day to my amazement, at the end of my first meeting, who should stand up and testify that he was saved but this very professor! Afterwards I went up to him. "How did it happen?" I asked. "After you had gone," he said, "I picked up the Bible you left me and my eye caught the words in John chapter 1: 'The day after', 'the next day', 'the day after'. This writer, I thought to myself, knows what he's talking about. He *saw* it all. It is like a diary. Then I thought, What if after all there *is* a God? I should be a fool not to believe in Him. You had told me I could pray even to the God whose very existence I doubted, so I knelt and prayed. I don't know what I expected, but as I prayed I *knew* there was a God. How I knew I cannot explain; I just knew it! Then the words of that eye-witness, John, came back to me. Since there is a God, I thought, then Jesus *could* only be His Son—and I was saved!"

AUGUST 6th

The Lord that delivered me out of the paw of the lion, and
out of the paw of the bear, he will deliver me out of the hand
of this Philistine. 1 Samuel 17. 37.

David was anointed king at Bethlehem, but immediately he returned to his ordinary sphere of life to prove
the Lord there. He went back to his flock, not to some special
royal training-school. It was "with the sheep" that Saul's
messengers found him; and when his turn came to confront
Goliath, the weapons he used against him were those tested
there. Of Saul's helmet and sword and mail he said, "I have
not proved them," and he put them off him again. Instead he
chose his shepherd's sling and the stones from the brook, "that
all this assembly may know that the Lord saveth not with
sword and spear".

There is no virtue in office alone. Mere status carries with
it no spiritual power. You need to meet the enemy in secret
before you can meet him in public. You need to be in tune
with the Spirit of God at home before you can reign abroad.
But this is a training-school open to every one of us.

AUGUST 7th

The sun rose upon him as he passed over Penuel, and he
halted upon his thigh. Genesis 32. 31.

Here at Peniel, met face to face by God, Jacob received the new name of Israel. Yet the narrative continues to
call him Jacob! There is reason in this. The truth is, of course,
that nobody can completely change in one night. Jacob him-

self was not conscious of any great change. He only knew he had met God, and that now he had a permanent limp.

It is legitimate for us to use Scripture to interpret our experiences, especially when God has met us in a distinctive way. But let us beware of using it to build up false ideas of perfection. God's Word adheres firmly to hard facts, for nothing hinders spiritual growth more than pretence. For Jacob, Peniel was not the touch of perfection; it was the beginning only of a new and transforming experience of God. "The sun rose upon him."

AUGUST 8th

By faith Jacob . . . worshipped, leaning upon the top of his staff. Hebrews 11. 21.

How striking that the New Testament writer should choose this mark of apparent weakness to depict Jacob's faith. For Penuel, with its crippling divine touch, had indeed spelled an end to the supplanter with all his superabundant natural energy. In his place there stood now this gracious prince with God—and worshipped.

I was sitting one day at supper with a young brother to whom the Lord had been speaking on this very question of our natural energy. He said to me, "It is a blessed thing when you know the Lord has met you and dealt with you in a fundamental way, and that disabling touch has been received." There was a plate of biscuits between us on the table, and I picked one up and broke it in half as though to eat it. Then, fitting the two pieces together again carefully, I said, "It looks all right, but it is never quite the same again, is it? When once your back is broken, you will yield ever after to the slightest touch from God."

AUGUST 9th

The angel which hath redeemed me from all evil, bless the lads. Genesis 48. 16.

Isaac and Jacob illustrate the objective and the subjective sides of Christian experience. Isaac is a type of free grace; he received everything. Jacob on the other hand received nothing from others. His character was formed through the discipline of having to toil for it all. Both blessed their sons prophetically, but how different were their prophecies! Isaac did not understand what he was doing. The recipients of his blessing were the reverse of what he intended. But Jacob *knew*. When Joseph protested that he was making a mistake, he answered, "I know, my son, I know." He called each son by name, and he exactly understood them and their future. He had known what it was to wait for God's salvation.

AUGUST 10th

They were all together in one place. Acts 2. 1.

When at the incarnation God visited His people, but a handful of them looked for the redemption of Israel. They believed God was going to act, and through them and because of them He acted. Then in Jesus' own lifetime multitudes followed Him, but again it was a much smaller group who protested: "To whom shall we go? Thou hast the words of eternal life." And once more, before His ascension He instructed His own to await the promise of the Father. This command could well have reached over five hundred brethren who saw Him alive after His passion; yet by Pentecost only one hundred and twenty were gathered in prayer to cooperate with God in His newest move. Where were the other three hundred and eighty? No doubt they all came in later. But *now* . . .?

In practice it seems to work out that God has always to move through a faithful remnant who, within the larger number and for the sake of God's purpose in the whole, will be utter in their obedience to Him *today*.

AUGUST 11th

When they heard that the Lord had visited the children of Israel, and that he had seen their affliction, then they bowed their heads and worshipped. Exodus 4.31.

No change had actually taken place in their condition. They had only been assured by Moses and Aaron that God had not forgotten them during those four hundred and more years. This assurance was enough. They bowed in worship.

We feel unable to worship God because we think He has forgotten us in our trial and left us to our own resources. We have been sick and have longed for healing; we have been out of employment for months and still cannot find a job; our domestic difficulties seem endlessly prolonged (though scarcely yet for 430 years!); those closest to us refuse to believe in the Lord, in spite of all our prayers; the same old harassing circumstances remain. How can we worship Him? Our lips are silenced—until we see. A day comes when we understand the ways of God, and at once we *know* He has not forgotten us. In that day the silent lips are opened, the resentful heads bowed. We acknowledge God's grace in everything and we adore His ways.

AUGUST 12th

*The love of God hath been shed abroad in our hearts
through the Holy Ghost which was given unto us.*
Romans 5. 5.

Because the Lord Jesus died on the Cross I have received forgiveness of sins; because He rose from the dead I
have received new life; because He has been exalted to the
right hand of the Father I have received the gift of the Spirit.
All is because of Him; nothing is because of me. Remission of
sins is not based on my merit but on His crucifixion, regeneration is not based on my merit but on His resurrection, and the
enduement with the Holy Spirit is not based on my merit but
on His exaltation. The Holy Spirit has been given to you and
me both to be the evidence that God's Son is in the glory, and,
by the power of divine love, to lead us there. By His witness
we know that Jesus of Nazareth, who was crucified by wicked
men nearly two thousand years ago, did not just die a
martyr's death but is exalted for us at the Father's right hand
in glory. Hallelujah!

AUGUST 13th

*The word of God is living, and active, and sharper than
any two-edged sword, and piercing even to the dividing of
soul and spirit.* Hebrews 4. 12.

Some of God's children lay great emphasis on
rightly dividing the word of truth. Indeed Scripture itself tells
us we are to do this (2 Timothy 2. 15), but it also tells us His
Word is to divide us. Where we may be wrong is in seeking to
divide His Word first, before we have allowed it to do its

work on us! Are we aware of this living, powerful character of God's Word? Does it deal with us like a sharp, two-edged sword? Or do we handle it as though it were just one more book to be studied and analysed?

The strange thing about Scripture is that it does not aim to make us understand doctrines in a systematic way. Perhaps we think it would have been better if Paul and the others had got together to provide a detailed handbook of Christian doctrines. But God did not permit this. How easily He could have settled some of our theological arguments, but it seems He loves to confuse those who only approach the Bible intellectually! He wants to preserve men from merely getting hold of doctrines. He wants His truth to get hold of them.

AUGUST 14th

While Peter yet spake these words, the Holy Ghost fell on all them who heard the word. Acts 10. 44.

God was always having to interrupt Peter! On the mount of transfiguration "while he was yet speaking" the Father spoke. "This is my beloved Son," He said. "Hear *him*"! Back in the house at Capernaum, when he had just committed his Lord to payment of the temple tax and was about to tell Him so, "Jesus spake first to him" to correct Peter's false ideas on the matter. And here in Caesarea, while Peter was still speaking, the Holy Spirit broke into the sermon with His mighty acts, so that Peter's six companions "were amazed", and so could be appealed to in support of his testimony on their return to Jerusalem. Father, Son and Holy Spirit each intervened to interrupt Peter. We may welcome any check upon our flow of words when it is God Himself who breaks in!

AUGUST 15th

Blessed are the pure in heart: for they shall see God. Matthew 5. 8.

Here is a heart-condition God requires for the fulfilment of His purposes of grace. Purity of heart simply means a state where there are no hindrances to seeing God. The kingdom of the heavens is here, so there is no reason why anyone should fail to see Him, *unless man himself puts up barriers.*

It is not necessary to place a dirty article in front of your eyes to prevent you seeing an object; a perfectly clean article will do just as well! The "clean heart" of the psalmist has to do with the removal of unclean things; the "pure heart" of the Sermon on the Mount has to do with the removal of all things, clean or unclean. Many have no right knowledge of God because they let their hearts run wild, so that they have numerous competing interests apart from God. Purity of heart corresponds to singleness of eye. It means that God is the exclusive object of attention. From such preoccupation there will be no loss. "Thy whole body shall be full of light."

AUGUST 16th

He shall give strength unto his king. 1 Samuel 2. 10.

The book of Judges is a record of revivals. The history of God's people is one of repeated backsliding, with God choosing one here, one there, as His instruments to bring recovery. But is this His real purpose for them? Are we today to expect another revival? Certainly our thoughts turn that way. But does God intend that, or something different?

God's eyes are towards a kingdom. He is planning for a King. The prophet Samuel becomes a link between the sorry history of the Judges and the ultimate fulness represented by David. He stands, the man of prayer, at the junction of the road to God's purpose. A great change is to take place and a kingdom be ushered in, and prayer will bridge the gap. Herein lies the wonder of Hannah's ministry. Her natural condition was no accident, but determined by God (1. 5). It brought her near to despair, yet with God in view she could not accept it as final. "O Lord of hosts!" she prayed, and in some amazing way her exercise of soul was harnessed to heaven's interests. The dearest thing in her life was dedicated in advance to those interests, and when the time came, given without regret to fulfil them.

AUGUST 17th

Seven days shalt thou tarry, till I come to thee, and shew thee what thou shalt do. 1 Samuel 10. 8.

Saul was tested on two points: faith and obedience. In a critical situation in Chapter 13 the question was, Would his faith allow him to wait for God? If you are driven into a corner and everything shouts that you should *do* something, then comes the test of whether you are carnal or spiritual. "*Till I come.*" Can the Lord count on us not to precipitate things until His hour strikes?

Again in Chapter 15 Saul was told to destroy Amalek utterly. But the bleating of sheep gave him away, for it is often the little things that betray us. Saul was attempting to judge between good and bad carnality, so as to bring something "good" in man and present it to God. That is no substitute for obedience; yet, "I have obeyed the voice of the Lord", he protested. Yes, the heart is deceitful. The Saul line of things is beyond improvement. God must have something altogether new, altogether different. He looks for one who will set his own judgment aside and be wholly governed by heaven. "But now thy kingdom shall not continue: the Lord hath sought him a man after his own heart."

AUGUST 18th

David therefore departed thence, and escaped to the cave of Adullam, . . . and there were with him about four hundred men. 1 Samuel 22. 1 f.

The cave represented the answer to a spiritual need. Saul had the office of king and a great following. His was all the machinery of government, and God in sovereignty recognized him, but you will not find God with Saul. It is David who is under the Spirit's anointing, and he must go with God into the wilderness. So the cave became his headquarters. To it there found their way a band of those who were weary of existing conditions, and he became their captain. They came to Adullam in desperation, because their need was met nowhere else.

David is a type of the Lord Jesus in His present rejection. Even today, multitudes are on their way to His retreat. They crave for the reality to be found where the Spirit rules. They come to Him and He owns them as His loyal band. It is a lonely way. It is always lonely to stand against the man-made system. But that nucleus, gathered to the Lord Jesus in this day of His rejection, will be very dear to Him when He comes to the throne.

AUGUST 19th

Praise him, O ye servants of the Lord. Ye that stand in the house of the Lord, in the courts of the house of our God. Psalm 135. 1f.

What a privilege to stand in praise before the Lord! It seems to me that today we always want to be moving on; we cannot stand still. So many things claim our attention that we are perpetually on the go. We cannot stop for a moment. But he who is spiritual knows how to stand still. He can stand before God in worship while God makes known to him His will. He can pause and await orders.

May I ask you, dear fellow-worker, is not all your work carried out to a schedule? And has it not to be done in great haste? Can you be persuaded to call a halt and stand a while before Him in praise? You will learn much that way.

AUGUST 20th

Your fathers ... served other gods. And I took your father Abraham from beyond the River, and led him throughout all the land of Canaan, and multiplied his seed. Joshua 24. 2 f.

Abraham was called and chosen, not just for himself but for his descendants, not merely to receive grace but to transmit grace to others. There had been men of faith before him, men like Abel, Enoch and Noah, who had nobly stood out as different from their fellows; but to judge from the record, they almost seem to have done so from birth. Abraham however was in his beginnings an idolator just like those around him. By himself, until God called him, he could not be ranked alongside those three.

Yet Matthew's Gospel opens with his name. Of all Old Testament names, his occurs most on the lips of Jesus. And this idolator was the man chosen to bring blessing to countless multitudes—chosen for no other reason than that God was pleased to choose him. There was nothing inherent in his character to suggest that through him such blessing should come to so many. God took him, led him and multiplied him. Cannot the same God do the same for you?

AUGUST 21st

But he, being full of the Holy Ghost, looked up steadfastly into heaven, and saw the glory of God, and Jesus standing on the right hand of God. Acts 7. 55.

Stephen's first words to the council were of God and His glory. "Brethren and fathers, hearken," he said: "The God of glory appeared unto our father Abraham. Then came he ... and dwelt in Haran." The man who sees that glory knows he must respond. He cannot do otherwise. Abraham responded, and through all the setbacks and discouragements of his pilgrimage the vision of God's glory carried him in triumph. Stephen set out first of all to remind his hearers of this.

They heard Stephen's testimony, and rejected it, only to become suddenly aware that he himself was beholding that of which he spoke! Full of the Holy Ghost, he looked up steadfastly "and saw the glory of God". He who appeared to Abraham and He whom Stephen saw were one and the same. There is no change in Him. And that same God, His splendour still undimmed, now carried Stephen through his own terrible crisis. What matters an extra stone or two to one who beholds the glory of God!

AUGUST 22nd

On this side of the river and on that was the tree of life,
bearing twelve manner of fruits, yielding its fruit every
month. Revelation 22. 2.

There is one River, not four as in Genesis, where two
of them, Hiddekel and Euphrates, were one day to become
scenes of sorrow for God's people. Here one river of life, full
of water, proceeds out of the throne, to make glad the city of
God.

And there is one Tree, yielding its fruit every month. There
is no fall, no barren winter, no need to store from last month's
supply. By it we shall go on knowing Christ with ever-fresh
knowledge, for in its different fruits we shall taste Him at all
points, not just at one.

River and Tree, Christ's fulness and Christ's ever-newness:
we cannot move without them. Wherever we go we must
carry them with us now—Christ's way of life to give light and
healing to the nations.

AUGUST 23rd

O send out thy light and thy truth; let them lead me: let
them bring me unto thy holy hill. Psalm 43. 3.

"Thy light and thy truth": the two are connected.
The truth is complete in Christ, but the need of our hearts is to
have God's light shed on it. For while the basis of all our
certainty is the *reality* of Christ's person and of His victorious
work, we still have, with God's help, to *see* this—to know the
glorious truth that He already reigns, not that He is going to.

What God does in us today is something already *done* in Christ. Our supreme need is to be shown this fact. All spiritual experience derives from the shedding of divine light upon eternal truth. Preached without light from God, truth remains but doctrine. With that light, it will transform you and me, so that the reality, found till now in Christ alone, begins to be seen also in what God is making us to become in Him. And this pathway leads right on to God's "holy hill".

AUGUST 24th

In thy light shall we see light. Psalm 36. 9.

His light may come to us in many ways. Some of us have known saints who really knew the Lord, and through praying with them or talking with them, in the light of God radiating from them, we have seen what we never saw before. I have met one such, who is now with the Lord, and I always think of her as a "lighted" Christian. If I did but walk into her room I was brought immediately to a sense of God. In those days I was very young, and had lots of plans and schemes for the Lord to sanction. With all these I came to her to try to persuade her; to tell her this or that was the thing to do. But before I could open my mouth she would perhaps say a few words in quite an ordinary way. Light dawned! It simply put me to shame. I realized that my doing and my scheming were all so natural, so full of man. For she lived for God alone, and such a one is bathed in a light that illumines others.

AUGUST 25th

Arise, O Lord, into thy resting place; thou, and the ark of thy strength. Psalm 132. 8.

Everything in the temple of Solomon was built anew—everything, that is, except the ark. There was a new altar, a new laver or sea, new curtains, tables, candlesticks and all else. Moreover, all was on a grander scale than in the tabernacle. Lavers and candlesticks were multiplied, and the dimensions of the structure and of everything within it were greater than before. Only the ark was still the same.

The tabernacle in the wilderness typified God's presence amid His pilgrim people; the much larger temple, His presence among them in the settled kingdom. And it is certain that in the Kingdom that is to come we shall have a greater appreciation of the sacrifice of Christ than we have now, yes, and a greater apprehension too of the Spirit's fulness. Yet the changeless ark reminds us that God's testimony concerning the person of His Son is eternally the same; it can never be enlarged or elaborated. Our own grasp of Him and of His work can grow. *He changes not.*

AUGUST 26th

For I, saith the Lord, will be unto her a wall of fire round about. Zechariah 2. 5.

To describe the great city of God in the Revelation, John starts from the wall, for it is the wall that delimits all that is His own. Walls suggest security and strength. They suggest also separation. It is separation from a world out of which he has been delivered that is one distinctive mark of a Christian. Satan abhors such clear delimitation. (He much prefers walls of partition between the saints!) In Ezra's day, as later in Nehemiah's, it was the rebuilding of Jerusalem's walls which provoked such violent hostility. What comfort therefore that the Lord Himself says: "*I* will be a wall to her"!

AUGUST 27th

The natural man receiveth not the things of the spirit of God: for they are foolishness unto him. 1 Corinthians 2. 14.

It has pleased God to say many things which leave room for misunderstanding, and not to explain them. Often in the Bible there seem to be conflicting statements, or statements that seem to violate the known facts of life, and it has pleased Him to leave them there. There are many scriptures we cannot clearly explain. Had we been writing we would have put things far more plainly, so that men should have before them all the doctrine in foolproof systematic order. *But would they have had the life?*

The mighty eternal truths of God are half obscured in Scripture so that the natural man may not lay hold of them. God has hidden them from the wise to reveal them to babes, for they are spiritually discerned. His Word is not a study book. It is intended to meet us in the course of our day-to-day walk in the Spirit and to speak to us there. It is designed to give us knowledge that is experimental because related to life. If we are trying through systematic theology to know God, we are absolutely on the wrong road.

AUGUST 28th

Be ye kind one to another, tenderhearted, forgiving each other, even as God also in Christ forgave you. Ephesians 4. 32.

If you forgive a brother, the reality of your forgiveness will minister life to the Body, quite apart from any expression of it. If you truly love a brother, that love will build up the Body, even though you may never tell him how you love him. I found myself once, at short notice, taking part on the platform in a large convention meeting in England where, unknown to me, a Japanese brother was to be one of the speakers. We had not met before—and our two countries were at war. I do not know what that brother felt, and we had opportunity for but a brief conversation. I only know that while he spoke I was aware of the love and fellowship of a brother in the Lord, a love that leaped over national barriers, and that did not demand words for its expression.

AUGUST 29th

Ye search the scriptures, . . . and these are they which bear witness of me. John 5. 39.

In the Old Testament there is not only law and song and prophecy; there is Christ. But *how* is He there? We see types of Christ and prophecies of Christ and Messianic psalms; but is He merely written about there, or is there something more?

Jesus affirms that Abraham rejoiced to see His day, and saw it (John 8. 56). Moses, at a critical point of decision, rejected Egypt's wealth in favour of the reproach of Christ (Hebrews

11. 23 ff.). We read of David's sighs and desires and praises, and we say: "That's David!" No, that is Christ. For David, in describing his own experiences, "spake of the resurrection of Christ" (Acts 2. 25 ff.). And Isaiah did not just pass on information given to him; he saw His glory and he spake of Him (John 12. 41). You cannot detach God from His servants. The life of Christ in them took them through certain experiences and they recorded them. In these many persons down the centuries Christ moved to express Himself, and the sum of the records is the Word of God, "the things concerning Himself".

AUGUST 30th

And she said unto him, I am the daughter of Bethuel. . . .
And the man bowed his head and worshipped the Lord.
Genesis 24. 24 ff.

Do you see what it means to worship God? When you are faced with some difficult task about which you have sought the Lord for help, and when thereafter things fall out as you asked, do you just rejoice in the prosperity of your way? Or worse, are you inclined to attribute some of it to your own ability, or to chance? It was not so with Abraham's servant. He did not congratulate himself on the fortunate turn events had taken. He did not even stop to talk with Rebekah. Without hesitation or embarrassment he bowed his head, and his lips formed the words: "Blessed be the Lord!" His instantaneous reaction was to adore the ways of God, and at each new turn of events he saw a new opportunity to do so. To be a true worshipper is to bring glory to God by offering Him instant praise and thanksgiving for everything we meet. For God orders all our ways so that we may bring to Him the worship He desires.

AUGUST 31st

*He saith unto them, Moses for your hardness of heart
suffered you to put away your wives: but from the beginning it hath not been so.* Matthew 19. 8.

To the Pharisees there seemed to be a discrepancy
between the teaching of Jesus that what God has joined together must not be sundered and the command of Moses
concerning divorce. Superficially of course there *is* a discrepancy; but there is no change in God. It is not that what
was first forbidden became lawful in His eyes later on, and
still later was forbidden again, as though God were capricious.
No, when Jesus says "From the beginning it hath not been
so", He affirms that, despite appearances, God's will is consistent. It has never altered. Here is a most important principle.
It is not God's permissions, but His directive will we need
always to discover. We should ask ourselves what was God's
purpose from the beginning. We need to see things as they
were when they proceeded in all their purity from the mind of
God, not as they have become because of His people's hardness of heart.

SEPTEMBER 1st

*O woman, great is thy faith; be it done unto thee even as
thou wilt.* Matthew 15. 28.

In the agony of her need this Canaanite woman had
cried: "Have mercy on me, O Lord, thou son of David!"
Was she not earnest in her prayer? Truly she was. Then was it
not the kind of prayer that might be expected to receive an
immediate answer? We would think so. Yet amazingly, Jesus
"answered her not a word" To her He seemed to have

nothing to say, but to the disciples' complaints about her He replied that His mission was to "the lost sheep of the house of Israel". That answer seems to have supplied her with the clue to a right approach to Him however. For He was "son of David" only to Israel. Others had no such claim upon Him. Realizing this, she changed the ground of her appeal, addressing Him now simply as Lord.

His first response to her had *seemed* like a rebuff. But in fact He was helping her to seek Him, not on the false ground of a privilege she had no claim to, but solely on the ground of un-merited grace. Her faith now met an instant response. She had found the key.

SEPTEMBER 2nd

He said unto her, For this saying go thy way; the devil is gone out of thy daughter. Mark 7. 29.

The question is sometimes asked: Does the exercise of a ministry of prayer, so vital to the Christian, call for utterance, or is it enough if we bear our burdens silently before God? I believe the answer is that if God gives a burden of prayer, He does in fact want it to be uttered. He wants audible expression given to it, however few and disjointed the words we may use. No burden can be discharged without this ex-pression. Even our Lord Himself in Gethsemane "offered up prayers and supplications with strong crying". It seems to me that in spiritual things there is an amazing link between faith and utterance. God not only takes account of what we believe, He takes account of what we say. The Syrophoenician woman spoke only a sentence, but as a result of this she returned to her house to find the devil gone!

SEPTEMBER 3rd

There builded he an altar unto the Lord. Genesis 12. 7.

It was where God had appeared to him that Abram built an altar. Until God appears to a man, that man does not on his own initiative offer Him his all. But the day God meets him, that day God has his life. Abram knew little of the doctrine of consecration, nor had he been urged by others to consecrate himself; which perhaps was well, for not all who preach consecration, I fear, are consecrated people, and many who understand the doctrine know little of the reality. But Abram had seen God, and so he built his altar. Catch a glimpse of Him and you are His for ever. Two thousand years of church history only go to confirm this.

SEPTEMBER 4th

Wherefore, brethren, give the more diligence to make your calling and election sure. 2 Peter 1. 10.

Spiritual wealth comes not from special gifts of grace on special occasions, but from unremitting divine activity in a human life over years of time. It is a grief to me to find brothers and sisters so dependent on special experiences that, between the periodic help these bring, they lapse into a life indistinguishable from that of the pagans around them. What a poverty-stricken state this reveals! They are laying in store no riches. Between the temporary lift they get from Christian meetings or other means of grace, they live a life of defeat. The life of the Spirit is not like that. Its wealth is not gained at the halting-places of life, but through the ceaseless operation of God's grace on the long stretch of the road between.

SEPTEMBER 5th

Flesh and blood hath not revealed it unto thee, but my Father which is in heaven. Matthew 16. 17.

The Church's foundation is not only Christ but the knowledge of Christ. The tragedy today is that many of us in the churches—indeed many so-called churches—lack such foundation. We do not know Him. To us He is a theoretical or doctrinal Christ, not a revealed Christ. But theory will not prevail against hell, which is what Jesus declares His Church is to do. Have we perhaps forgotten what we are for? Visiting Western homes I have sometimes seen a beautiful porcelain plate, not put to use on the table, but wired and hung up to the wall as a treasured ornament. Many, it seems to me, think of the Church like that, as something to be admired for the perfection of its form. But no, God's Church is for use, not decoration. An appearance of life may seem to suffice when conditions are favourable, but when the gates of hell come out against us, we know well enough that what we each need above all is a God-given vision of His Son. It is first-hand knowledge that counts in the hour of testing.

SEPTEMBER 6th

Abide in me, and I in you. As the branch cannot bear fruit of itself, except it abide in the vine; so neither can ye, except ye abide in me. John 15. 4.

These familiar words remind us that it is God who has placed us in Christ. We are there, and we are told to *stay* there! It was God's own act, and we are to abide by it. "Abide in me, and I in you." This is a double sentence: a command matched by a promise. That is to say, there is an objective and a subjective side to God's working, and the subjective depends on the objective; the "I in you" is the outcome of our abiding in Him. We need to guard against being over-anxious about the subjective side of things, as though a branch of the vine should strive to produce grapes of a particular size or colour. We need to dwell upon the objective— "Abide in me"—and let God take care of the outcome. And this He has undertaken to do. The character of the fruit is always determined by the Vine.

SEPTEMBER 7th

At midnight there is a cry, Behold the bridegroom! Come ye forth to meet him. Matthew 25. 6.

It was the bridegroom's tarrying that brought to light the state of the virgins. How can I be prepared for the Lord's coming? There are some of us who would have been ready had He come five years ago, but who would not if He came today. It is good to be prepared should He come now, but it is no less important to keep prepared, should He tarry. Can we wait and still be ready? Some people can wait three days, but not three years. Some could hang on for three years at a pinch, but they may be required to watch for thirty. For consider this: if the bridegroom had come before midnight, all the virgins would have been wise! It was His delay which exposed their folly. May God preserve me from becoming foolish with the passing years! One thing only can insure me against the test of time: His Spirit's fulness. Let me but know His constant filling and there will not lack oil in my lamp when that great midnight cry goes forth.

SEPTEMBER 8th

Nay: but as captain of the host of the Lord am I now come.
Joshua 5. 14.

Faced with the task of leading Israel against this land of seven strong nations, it were little wonder if Joshua were to feel overwhelmed. But here by Jericho he was given this vision. A Man with a drawn sword stood before him. "Art thou for us, or for our adversaries?" he inquired, and the answer came back, an uncompromising "Nay". He was neither for the one side nor the other. He had come "as captain".

Praise God, this is His purpose, to take His place as Captain of His host. We want everything to circle round us and serve our interests, but God will not have it so. He does not stand in the midst of the conflict giving a little help here or there. For us the question at issue is not one of receiving help, but of accepting leadership. You do not know God if you think He can occupy a subordinate position in the battle. His place is to lead. Only then will you know what it means to have His sword drawn on your behalf.

SEPTEMBER 9th

Behold, I am with thee, . . . for I will not leave thee, until I have done that which I have spoken to thee of. Genesis 28. 15.

Here at Bethel, in spite of Jacob's spiritual state, God had no word of rebuke for him. We certainly would have berated him soundly! And God is holy; He had no liking for

Jacob's deceptions. Yet He did not reprove him. What use would it have been? Jacob could not change himself, and God did not therefore exhort him to do so. But what was impossible to Jacob God could do, and His words reveal His absolute confidence in Himself. "I will not leave thee until I have done . . ." He knew that His servant could not escape His hand, and that the Jacob who would return years later to Bethel would be a very different man. "Behold, I am with thee." This is our comfort.

SEPTEMBER 10th

By faith Noah, being warned of God concerning things not seen as yet, moved with godly fear, prepared an ark to the saving of his house; through which he condemned the world, and became heir of the righteousness which is according to faith. Hebrews 11. 7.

We cannot speak of "baptismal regeneration", but we may speak of "baptismal salvation", salvation from the *cosmos* or world-system. We are involved in Satan's world-system. To be saved is to make our exit from his world into God's. In the Cross of our Lord Jesus the world has been crucified unto us and we unto the world. This is the figure developed by Peter when he writes of the eight souls who were "saved through water" (1 Peter 3. 20). Entering into the ark, Noah and those with him stepped by faith out of that old corrupt world into a new one. It was not so much that they were personally not drowned, but that they were *out* of that corrupt system. That is salvation. When you are baptized you go down into the water and your world, in figure, goes down with you. You come up in Christ, but your world is drowned.

SEPTEMBER 11th

Look unto me, and be ye saved, all the ends of the earth.
Isaiah 45. 22.

How aptly this describes the experience of the dying thief! All history had pointed forward to the Cross of Christ. Now the event itself was being enacted before men's eyes, and this criminal was a key witness. A model sinner, he was receiving a model punishment. We must conclude therefore that his was a model conversion. Yet I ask you, did he recognize Jesus as Saviour? Consider his words: "Remember me when thou comest into thy kingdom" (Luke 23. 42). What did the Lord reply? He did not explain the atonement to this man, telling him his punishment was just, but that He, Jesus, was dying in his stead as a sacrifice for sin. To us it would have seemed an excellent opportunity to announce the truths of redemption; but no, He answered only, "Today shalt thou be with me in paradise." For the thief saw dimly who Jesus was: that through suffering unjustly, He would reign and have a kingdom. Beholding at his side the Lord of all the earth, he cried out *to Him*, and that was enough.

SEPTEMBER 12th

I had heard of thee by the hearing of the ear; but now mine eye seeth thee. Job 42. 5.

Sound doctrine can inflate us, making us proud of our knowledge or our opinions. Or we can forget the truth by having it knocked out of us by skilled argument or third-degree methods. But vision is revolutionary. Beside it everything else becomes small. Once see the Lord and we shall never forget Him. With the attacks of Satan increasing and the counsel of friends failing us, it is only the inner knowledge of God that will make us stand in the testing time.

For a year or two after my conversion I used to fear lest a modernist or an atheist should come along and prove to me that the Bible was faulty and unreliable. I thought, if he did, that would finish everything. My faith would be lost; and I *wanted* to believe. But now all is peace. If all of them came, and if they brought as many arguments against the Bible as there are bullets in the armouries of Europe, my answer would be one and the same. "There is a great deal of reason in what you say—but I know my God. That is enough."

SEPTEMBER 13th

Let us draw near with a true heart in fulness of faith, having our hearts sprinkled from an evil conscience. Hebrews 10. 22.

When we enter the Most Holy Place, on what ground dare we enter but by the precious Blood of Christ? But I have to ask myself, am I really seeking the way into the presence of God by the Blood or by something else? What do I mean when I say, "by the Blood"? Simply that I recognize my sins, that I confess that I have need of cleansing, and that I come to God on the basis of the finished work of the Lord Jesus. I approach God through His merit alone, and never on the basis of my attainment; never, for example, on the ground that I have been extra kind or patient today, or that today I have done something for the Lord.

I may be mistaken, but I fear some of us are thinking in terms such as these: "Today I have been a little more careful; today I have been doing a little better; so today I can approach God and can pray better!" No, no, *no*! A clear conscience is *never* based upon our attainment; it can only be based on the atoning work of the Lord Jesus in the shedding of His Blood.

SEPTEMBER 14th

This is nothing else save the sword of Gideon the son of Joash, a man of Israel: into his hand God hath delivered Midian, and all the host. Judges 7. 14.

It is the means it pleased God to use to reassure His servant that is so arresting. Here was this vast invading army, like locusts for multitude, and Gideon had been instructed progressively to disband his own forces. It seemed absurd to expect the three hundred that remained to overthrow this Midianite host, and Gideon seems to have had no assurance regarding the issue. It was in this state of uncertainty that he ventured into the enemy camp.

Praise God, when we have no way out it is always an easy matter for Him to open a way. That little band of men was indeed to be His instrument for the deliverance of His people, and His servant, in his own dilemma, was to hear the assuring news in the way most calculated to stir his faith, namely from the prophetic lips of one of his foes. Fear, he learned, had already struck them. No wonder he worshipped!

SEPTEMBER 15th

Ye shall not be as the hypocrites. Matthew 6.5.

Too many of us are caught *acting* as Christians. We live a "spiritual" life, talk "spiritual" language, adopt "spiritual" attitudes, but we are doing the whole thing ourselves. Perhaps indeed we are doing it fairly well, but it is the effort involved that should warn us something is wrong. We force ourselves to refrain from this, from that, from the other, and what a strain it all is! Do you ever have to talk a language not your own? If so you know what I mean. Try as you will it does not flow spontaneously. You have to force yourself to talk that way. But when it comes to speaking your own language, nothing could be easier. You speak it effortlessly, without conscious thought. Its very spontaneity reveals to everyone *what you are*.

Nothing is so hurtful to a Christian life as play-acting, nothing so blessed as when our words, our prayers, our very demeanour, all become a spontaneous expression of the life of Christ our wonderful Lord.

SEPTEMBER 16th

He hath said unto me, My grace is sufficient for thee: for my power is made perfect in weakness. 2 Corinthians 12. 9.

It is significant that Paul says very little about the nature of the "visions and revelations of the Lord" alluded to in this chapter. It would not be profitable, he says, to boast of them, and only against his desires and under strong compulsion does he mention the experiences of "fourteen years ago". Fourteen years! And yet with many of us, directly we have something from God, the whole of Shanghai knows it! To suppress it even for two years would be a feat. But Paul, even after so long, does not tell us *what* that vision was, save that it was a further seeing of Christ. He tells us however of the subsequent "thorn in the flesh" and of God's gracious answer to his prayer. It is that answer, not the visions, that has brought strength to so many.

SEPTEMBER 17th

Ye meant evil against me; but God meant it for good.
Genesis 50. 20.

God had a special work for Joseph to do: to save Israel from famine and death. His ways with His servant were most exceptional, but in the end Joseph could say to his brethren: "God sent me before you to preserve life." He understood. The question is, do we? Not only when we are consciously serving Him, but from our earliest beginnings God's hand is upon us. His foreknowledge prepared our circumstances even before we were born. He determined whose child we should be, though sometimes we may feel we have been born into the wrong family! Some of us approve of our parents but would like perhaps to change our brothers and sisters, or our other relatives! Joseph could have felt this, and with reason, for they plotted evil against him. But the whole road is prepared for us by God. He *means* it all, and He means it *for good*. If we have not seen God's hand at work in His choices, we have lost a great opportunity to bring Him praise.

SEPTEMBER 18th

The way of an eagle in the air. Proverbs 30. 19.

Consider the birds. If you could ask them whether they were not afraid of the law of gravity, how would they reply? They would say: "We never heard the name of Newton. We know nothing about his law. We fly because it is the law of our life to fly." Not only is there in them a life with the power of flight, but that life has a law which enables these living creatures quite spontaneously to overcome the law of gravity. Yet gravity remains. If you get up early one morning when the cold is intense and the snow thick on the ground, and there is a dead sparrow in the courtyard, you are reminded at once of the persistence of that law. But while birds live they overcome it, and the life within them is what dominates their consciousness. Yes, the law of the spirit of life in Christ Jesus *has* made me free from the law of sin and death!

SEPTEMBER 19th

They entered . . . into the synagogue . . . and so spake that a great multitude both of Jews and of Greeks believed. Acts 14. 1.

When we stand up and speak, folk detect at once whether we stress doctrine or life. If it is the former, we never run risks. We keep carefully within the limits of our doctrinal scheme, in order to be absolutely safe and to avoid all possible chance of misunderstanding. We present our reasons in logical order, and by a process of induction arrive at our incontrovertible conclusions. But if it is life we are stressing, our approach will be very different. We shall be far less concerned with technical correctness, for we ourselves have known conditions through which mere doctrine could never carry us. If only we can present Christ in His living Person to our hearers, and leave them with Him, we know our object will be achieved.

SEPTEMBER 20th

After these things the word of the Lord came unto Abram in a vision, saying, Fear not, Abram: I am thy shield and thy exceeding great reward. Genesis 15. 1.

When God says "Fear not" it is because He detects either fear or doubt in His servant's heart. Note the events that have just preceded His words here. Abram, having received from Melchizedek bread and wine, seems to have found it easy to refuse the proffered rewards of the king of Sodom. Once home again, however, doubts and questions may well have crowded into his mind. Was it wise to have made so uncompromising a refusal of all help? Had his downrightness made him new enemies?

Thank God, to every doubt there is a divine assurance. "The word of the Lord came to Abram." As to his fears? *God* would be to him a protecting shield. As to the future? He offered *Himself*, no less, as Abram's superlative reward. How Abram must have thanked God he had not after all let himself be seduced by Sodom's pitiful substitute for this!

SEPTEMBER 21st

He that walketh in darkness, and hath no light, let him
trust in the name of the Lord, and stay upon his God.
Isaiah 50. 10.

When we find ourselves thrown into darkness, the
one great danger is that we shall start kindling fires (verse 11),
encircling ourselves with our own pale flames in the hope that
they will give us light by which to walk. "I have thought
things over; I have put two and two together; I feel con-
fident that . . .; my judgment is . . .;" such thoughts and
feelings as these are no source of light. They are but fire-
brands. Put them in the light of God and their conclusions are
seen to be neither deep enough nor clear enough. In the end
we shall but "lie down in sorrow". If it is confusion we want,
by all means let us look to such expedients. But darkness will
never be dispelled by men's fires. Light is from God alone.
Look up to Him! Even when all here is darkness, there is light
there. And "in thy light shall we see light".

SEPTEMBER 22nd

All the multitude sought to touch him. Luke 6. 19.

None of us can fathom the mysterious ways of God,
nor prescribe for Him how He shall work. There was a
Chinese boy who, when he was twelve years old, was taken
by his mother to worship in a temple up in the hills. As he
stood with her before the shrine, he looked at the idol, and he
thought: "You are too ugly and dirty to be worshipped. I
don't believe you can save me. What is the sense in wor-
shipping you?" But out of respect for his mother he joined in
the ceremony, and after it was over his mother got into her

chair to be carried down the mountain. Then he slipped away to the back of the temple and found there an open space. Looking up to heaven he said, "O God, whoever You are, I do not believe You can dwell in that dirty shrine. You are too big. I do not know how to find You, but I put myself in Your hands; for sin is very strong, and the world pulls. I commit myself to You, whoever You may be." Thirty years later I met him and told him the Gospel. He said, "I have met the Lord Jesus for the first time today, but this is the second time that I have touched God. Something happened to me long ago on that mountain top."

"And as many as touched him were made perfectly whole." God does not always explain to us how.

SEPTEMBER 23rd

He put the staves into the rings on the sides of the ark, to bear the ark. Exodus 37. 5.

The ark of testimony had no fixed platform. In the entire description of the Tabernacle, no mention is made of the floor beneath it, for of course it was the same desert soil as was trodden by the feet of every Israelite. And *our* testimony as Christians is what we are proving of Christ Himself in *our* daily walk. Moreover, just as the staves ensured that the ark was ever ready to be borne forward, so our testimony can never be static, but always mobile, fresh, vital. I mean this in the sense, not of something quickly conjured up when a need arises, but rather of an always ready, always fresh evidence of what God can do. Christ, and not in the first place what we say about Him, is the testimony we bear on our pilgrimage, and every step of the journey brings us new discoveries of Him.

SEPTEMBER 24th

We, who are many, are one body in Christ and severally members one of another. Romans 12. 5.

This concept of Jesus and His people as a body and its members was bound up with the very conversion and calling of Saul of Tarsus. The Lord's first words to him, "I am Jesus whom thou persecutest," stressed the fact that in touching His own, Saul was touching Him. In a remarkable way they heralded therefore the great revelation that was to be given him of the mystery of the Church. But the Lord did not leave the matter there. He did not allow him to stay with the heavenly mystery. The command that immediately followed came right down to the practical consequences of such a revelation. "Rise, and enter into the city, and it shall be told thee what thou must do." *It shall be told thee.* He must await instructions from those he hated! Apart from the very disciples he had set himself to destroy, Saul would be helpless; he would never know.

SEPTEMBER 25th

Our citizenship is in heaven; from whence also we wait for a Saviour, the Lord Jesus Christ. Philippians 3. 20.

Though we may work our way across the Atlantic or the Pacific, we can never work our way from earth to heaven. Heaven is not a place the Church will reach at some future date. The Church *is* there. Heaven is both her origin and her abode, but not her destination. And since this is so, the question of striving to reach heaven can never arise. This statement may appear extreme, I readily admit, but it is true. Oh to see afresh the wonders of our heavenly calling! That calling does not beckon us to heaven; it makes known to us that we belong there and are there! So we Christians are not working our way heavenward. We are citizens now of heaven, with all our affections firmly set there.

SEPTEMBER 26th

Thou didst hide these things from the wise and understanding, and didst reveal them unto babes. Matthew 11. 25.

Shortly after my conversion I went out preaching in the villages. I had had a good education and was well-versed in the Scriptures, so I considered myself thoroughly capable of instructing the village folk, among whom many were illiterate women. But after several visits I discovered that, despite their illiteracy, those women had an intimate knowledge of the Lord. I knew the Book they haltingly read; they knew the One of whom the Book spoke. I had much in myself; they had much in the Spirit. And it had not yet dawned on me that, apart from the discipline of the Cross, what I had could well prove a handicap to the Holy Spirit's working. How many Christian teachers today are teaching others, as I was then, very largely in the strength of their carnal equipment! But thank God, He reveals Himself to babes!

SEPTEMBER 27th

Sanctify in your hearts Christ as Lord. I Peter 3. 15.

The reason why so many Christians do not experience the power of the Spirit is that they lack reverence for Him. And they lack reverence because they have not had their eyes opened to the solemn fact of His indwelling presence. The fact is incontrovertible, but they have not seen it. Why do some of God's children live victorious lives while others are in a state of constant defeat? The difference is not accounted for by the presence or absence of the Spirit (for He dwells with every child of God) but by this, that some *know* His indwelling and others do not, and that consequently some recognize the divine ownership of their lives while others are still their own masters. Discovery of the fact that his heart is God's dwelling-place will revolutionize the life of any Christian.

SEPTEMBER 28th

While we were yet sinners, Christ died for us. Romans 5. 8.

Seeing the price of our redemption, how can we do other than give ourselves to Him? "By the mercies of God I beseech you," pleads Paul in Romans 12. Throughout the preceding eleven chapters he has recounted them, divine mercies all the way. Love led Christ to die that we might walk in newness of life. That same love of Christ draws us back to Him again. Faced by love so utterly selfless, it is harder to withhold than to offer ourselves to Him. To be for years a

Christian without total dedication to God is a wholly astounding thing; for were we not bought with a measureless price? Our willing choice therefore is to glorify God in our bodies and spirits, "which are God's" (1 Corinthians 6. 19 f.). This is His right, not a favour we are showing Him. I am not my own. Dare I purloin what is His? "Lord, all I have and am and hope for—all is Thine!"

SEPTEMBER 29th

He that cometh after me is mightier than I; . . . he shall baptize you with the Holy Ghost and with fire. Matthew 3. 11.

God only gives good gifts to His children. Unfortunately we are apt to esteem them lightly because of their sheer abundance. The Old Testament saints, who were less favoured than we are, could appreciate more readily the preciousness of this gift of the outpoured Spirit. In their day it was a gift given only to the select few, chiefly to priests, judges, kings and prophets, whereas now it is the portion of every child of God. Think! we mere nonentities who trust in Christ can have resting upon us the same Spirit who rested upon Moses the friend of God, upon David the beloved king, and upon Elijah the mighty prophet. "Among them that are born of women," said Jesus, "there hath not arisen a greater than John the Baptist: yet he that is but little in the kingdom of heaven is greater than he."

SEPTEMBER 30th

There is that scattereth, and increaseth yet more. Proverbs
11. 24.

God's principle of government in material things is
the principle of the manna, that "he that gathered much had
nothing over, and he that gathered little had no lack" (Exodus
16. 18 and 2 Corinthians 8. 14 f.). This means that if he that
has gathered little is to have no lack, anyone who has gathered
much must be willing to have nothing over. Some of us have
proved in experience the preciousness of this. When we bear
the burden for those who gather little, God sees to it that we
gather much; but if instead we think merely of our own needs,
the very utmost we can hope for is to gather little and have no
lack.

It is a privilege to be able to help our brethren in the Lord,
even to the extent of the greater part of our income. Those
who have only learned to take seldom receive; but those who
have learned to give are always receiving and have always
more to give. The more you spend on others, the more your
income will increase; the more you try to save, the more you
will be troubled by "rust" and "thieves".

OCTOBER 1st

*God remembered Abraham, and sent Lot out of the midst of
the overthrow.* Genesis 19. 29.

As soon as he understood that God was about to
execute judgment on Sodom, Abraham began to pray. It is
most instructive to see how he prayed. He did not merely
plead with God to spare the city. No, he based his appeal on
God's character. He laid hold upon the fact that He is a

righteous God. That was the secret of his prayer. In deep humility and with great earnestness he put to Him question after question. His questions were his requests, and all were based on the righteousness of God. After his final request, we are told, "the Lord went his way". Some people hold that Abraham should have continued asking. But he knew God, and above all he knew the secret of prayer. His intercession could save his kinsman because it was rightly based. When God overthrew the cities He "delivered righteous Lot" (2 Peter 2. 7).

OCTOBER 2nd

Remember Lot's wife. Whosoever shall seek to gain his life shall lose it: but whosoever shall lose his life shall preserve it. Luke 17. 32 f.

If I mistake not, this is the one passage in the New Testament that tells of our reaction to the rapture call. In that moment we shall discover our real heart's treasure. If it is the Lord Himself, there will be no backward look. It is so easy to become more attached to the gifts of God than to the Giver—and even, I may add, to the work of God than to God Himself. But he that is on the housetop is not to go back for his goods. Let me illustrate. I am engaged in writing a book. I have finished eight chapters and I have another nine to write, about which I am seriously exercised before the Lord. Now, suppose the call to "come up hither" were to come and my reaction were to be, "What about my book?" Is it not possible that that precious thing which I am doing downstairs in the house, as it were, might be enough to pin me down, a peg that could hold me to the earth? The question at issue is always, Where is my heart?

OCTOBER 3rd

It is God that worketh in you both to will and to work, for his good pleasure. Philippians 2. 13.

Now that I am in Christ, God's moral demands have not altered, but it is no longer I who meets them. Praise God, He who is the Lawgiver on the Throne is now also the Law-keeper in my heart. He who gave the Law Himself keeps it. He makes the demands, but He also meets them. While we were trying to do it all, He could do nothing. It was because we were struggling to achieve it that we failed and failed. The trouble with us was that we were weak enough not to do the will of God, but not yet weak enough to keep out of things altogether! Only utter disillusion can throw men back in despair upon the God who is ready to do it all.

OCTOBER 4th

This is the boldness which we have toward him, that, if we ask anything according to his will, he heareth us. 1 John 5. 14.

Faith only operates freely within the province of the will of God. Outside that will we may cry, believe, act in faith, and a great deal more, without perceptible result; God is not backing us. Trying to believe along some line of our own, we shall only prove that mountains of faith cannot remove a single mustard seed of difficulty! God will not be responsible for what we undertake on the basis of our own good intentions. His power is invested in His will. Get things right there, and we may have boldness in the face of the biggest testings. For "he heareth us".

OCTOBER 5th

You . . . by the power of God are guarded through faith.
I Peter 1, 5.

There is a condition attached to God's keeping power. We are guarded *through faith*. Unless we trust Him He cannot guard us. To know His safe-keeping we must believe whole-heartedly in His promises. If we harbour doubts about our security in face of temptation, are we not discrediting His ability to keep us? For it is not we who have to grapple with Satan's enticements. Every morning when we rise, we should say to Him: "I thank Thee for guarding me yesterday. I do not know what temptations may befall me today nor how I shall overcome them, but I trust Thee again to see me through." Rely implicitly on Him, our God of power. Then, however unpredictable the evil one's fiery darts, something amazingly wards them off. It is the shield of faith.

OCTOBER 6th

The priest's lips should keep knowledge, and they should seek the law at his mouth. Malachi 2. 7.

It is possible that much so-called revival is on a wrong basis. Spiritual gifts are displayed, but without a ministration of Christ, and that is like having many utensils, but nothing to use them for. But it is worse, for without Christ, gifts are not only empty; they may also be deceptive. Some of them at least can be simulated in a way that a ministry of Christ can never be. What matters to the Lord's people is not our gifts of preaching or prayer or what-have-you, but the personal knowledge of Christ that we convey by them. In a hospital two nurses may use exactly similar spoons, but what they give in those spoons is the important thing; one may give costly and curative medicine, the other a mere palliative. It is *what* we minister that counts.

OCTOBER 7th

Ye have heard that it was said of them of old time . . . but I say unto you . . . Matthew 5. 21 f.

Bondage to law may be defined as a rigid adherence to a bygone code of life that leaves us unready to follow the Lord's speaking in the present. We see the law as a standard of living; but it is a fixed standard. When we were youngsters at school our gymnastic teacher lowered or raised the rope for the high-jump according to our age and ability. The standard was subject to adjustment, and left us scope for development. But the law's standard is rigid. It leaves no room for advance beyond a given point.

"But I say unto you . . ." These words contain a principle for all time. I have heard people dispose of an argument with "Oh, that matter was settled in Calvin's (or Wesley's, or Darby's) day!" But their days are "old time", and so are your yesterday and mine. If I do what I did a month ago because to-day the Lord leads me to do it, that is life; but if I do it because He led me to a month ago, that is law. The law can be a week old or centuries old; but the leading of the Spirit can never be twenty-four hours old. The vital question is, do we know the freshness of today's walk with Him?

OCTOBER 8th

She of her want did cast in all that she had, even all her living. Mark 12. 44.

Today we talk of "clean money" and "dirty money" but in God's sight there is only "the mammon of unrighteousness". To test this you have only to ask yourself whether money leads you to God or away from Him. You cannot serve God and mammon. How then is it possible to take this that has served the interests of Satan and use it to build up the kingdom of God? What is needed to sever the connection that binds Caesar and that which bears His image?

If your money is to come out of the world, then *you* will have to come out of the world. Merely offering money to God's treasury will not of itself change the character of what you offer. Unless your life goes out with it, your money cannot be released from Satan's kingdom to God's. Paul says of the Macedonians that "first they gave their own selves to the Lord". Today, whereas in terms of money Satan's resources are unlimited, the hard cash effectively in God's hands is limited by the number of people devoted to Him. Make sure you instantly convert every dollar you earn to the currency of the Sanctuary. See to it that it is scored off Satan's books and transferred to God's account. How? Don't send it—*bring* it to Him.

OCTOBER 9th

A friend of publicans and sinners. Luke 7. 34.

Since I saw the Saviour as Friend of sinners I have seen many unusual and difficult people brought to Him. I remember once a young woman came and attacked me, saying that she did not want to be saved. She said she was young and intended to have a good time, and had no wish to leave her ways of sin, nor the least desire for salvation. After she had more or less raved at me for a while, I said, "Shall we pray?" "What on earth should I pray?" she replied scornfully. I said, "I can't be responsible for your prayer, but I will pray first, and then you can tell the Lord Jesus all that you have been saying to me." "Oh, I couldn't do that!" she said, somewhat taken aback. "Yes, you can," I replied. "Don't you know He is the Friend of sinners?" This touched her. She did pray—a very unorthodox prayer—but from that hour the Lord began to work in her heart, for within a few days' time she was gloriously saved.

OCTOBER 10th

Cast thy burden upon the Lord, and he shall sustain thee.
Psalm 55. 22.

Many Christians cannot be used of God in a prayer ministry because they are over-burdened. They have let their burdens accumulate instead of seeking relief in prayer, and ultimately they are so crushed by the weight of them that they cannot pray at all.

Suppose you intended asking someone to help you with a certain task, but found his hands were already full. Would it not be useless to invite his aid? In the same way, if you are weighed down by the thing God has already committed to you, how can He commit to you anything further? This ministry of prayer requires a liberated spirit, or the work of God will be seriously hampered. Would you be an instrument free and ready to hand for Him to use? Seek then the spiritual emancipation that comes from casting your burden on God.

OCTOBER 11th

The eye cannot say to the hand, I have no need of thee.
1 Corinthians 12. 21.

In our early days in Shanghai I confess I was always trying to force up the level of the meetings, especially the prayer meetings, to a certain high standard. Consequently I was very dissatisfied with the way some of the brothers prayed. I felt quite bad about it, and said so. How wrong I was!

For, some time later, the Lord laid me aside and I was in real physical need. I prayed hard, but my strong, fighting prayers seemed to get me nowhere. At length the Lord seemed to say to me, "You think certain of the brothers are very weak in prayer. Invite them to come and pray for you in your need." It was a challenge. I sent for those very same brothers, and they came, knelt down, and prayed. For the first time in my life I appreciated their simple, straightforward petitions. What is more, the Lord heard them. I was raised up!

OCTOBER 12th

Thy kingdom come. Thy will be done, as in heaven, so on earth. Matthew 6. 10.

We are to pray this. "Thy kingdom come!" If His kingdom would come of itself, we should not have been given that command. But God's people are to pray, for His work is done in response to their cry. "Thy will be done!" Yes, but where? "On earth", for this is the only place where today God's will is not done. Then how can God's kingdom be brought down here? By the created will, in union with the Uncreated Will, seeking the displacement of the rebellious will of the devil. For prayer is always three-sided. It involves someone prayed to, someone prayed for, and someone prayed against; and on earth there *is* someone to pray against—a will that is opposed to God's. Against that rebellious will, God will not act alone. He awaits our prayers. The Lord's Prayer is not just a model prayer for me; it is the revelation of God's heart.

OCTOBER 13th

Shall not God avenge his elect which cry to him day and night? Luke 18. 7.

Suppose a man somehow gets into your house and occupies it without your authority. What do you do? You go to the magistrate, and, appealing to the law of the land, you get a verdict against him. You return armed with a court order, and you turn him out. He may be fortunate not to go out in chains! But the situation in this world is no different. God's "statute book" has already ruled against this world's illegal occupant. He is to go! What matters it that to Satan the law of the Kingdom of heaven is an alien law? Calvary has established the superiority of that Kingdom. At the Cross, Christ overthrew Satan's whole legal standing. Now it is the Church's task to see that other law put into effect. Crying to God like the widow in the parable, "Avenge me of my adversary!" she is to obtain the order for his eviction, and throw him out. God waits for that cry.

OCTOBER 14th

By what power, or in what name, have ye done this?
Acts 4. 7.

Our eyes must be opened to see the mighty change wrought by the ascension. The name of Jesus certainly establishes the identity of the One in the throne with the Carpenter of Nazareth, but it goes further than that. It represents the power and dominion before which every knee in heaven and earth and beneath the earth must bow. Even the Jewish leaders recognized that there could be this kind of significance in a mere name, when they asked this question of the disciples concerning the lame man's healing.

Today the name tells us that God has committed all authority to His Son, so that in the very name itself there is power. But further, not only is it His, but it is "given among men". He has placed that authority in our hands for us to use. In three passages in His last discourse the Lord Jesus repeats the words "ask in my name". What confidence He must place in us to say, "Whatsoever ye shall ask in my name, that will I do"!

OCTOBER 15th

The throne of my lord king David. 1 Kings 1. 37.

"King David" they called him with affection, for he was every inch a king. He was a king in the wilderness when as shepherd of his father's sheep he put a lion to flight in the name of the Lord. Later when Goliath threatened Israel and even Saul trembled, not to mention his people, David remained unafraid. There is no fear in the heart of a king. But above all, when as a fugitive from Saul he suddenly found his pursuer at his mercy, he resolutely refused to strike the blow that could have brought him quick relief. This was true kingship, for he who cannot control his own spirit is no king. A true king is king under all circumstances. He reigns everywhere.

OCTOBER 16th

Strengthened with all power, according to the might of his glory, unto all patience and longsuffering with joy. Colossians 1. 11.

Apostleship has its credentials. The signs of an apostle will never be lacking where there is a true divine commission. There was abundant evidence of the genuineness of Paul's. "In nothing am I behind the very chiefest apostles," he writes in 2 Corinthians 12. "Truly the signs of an apostle were wrought among you in all patience, in signs and wonders, and mighty deeds." From this we infer that endurance is first among the proofs of spiritual power. It is the ability to endure steadfastly under continuous pressure that tests the reality of our call as the Lord's "sent ones". Patience and longsuffering with joy are to be found only in those who know what it is to be "strengthened with all power according to the might of his glory".

OCTOBER 17th

*The men took of their provision, and asked not counsel at
the mouth of the Lord.* Joshua 9. 14.

Sin before God is of two kinds. One is the sin of re-
fusing to obey when He issues orders; the other is the sin of
going ahead when He has issued none. The one is rebellion:
not doing what the Lord has commanded. The other is presumption: doing what He has not required. How much of our
work for Him has been based on a clear command of the Lord,
and how much simply on the ground that it was a good thing
to do? We think that if only our conscience does not forbid a
thing, or if it commends itself to us as positively good, that is
reason enough to go ahead and do it. Brothers and sisters, do
you not think that any servant should await his Master's
orders before setting out to serve Him?

OCTOBER 18th

*Thou, why dost thou judge thy brother? or thou again,
why dost thou set at nought thy brother? for we shall all
stand before the judgment seat of God.* Romans 14. 10.

Two things are here forbidden to us: "judging" and
"setting at nought", an outward act and an inner attitude. I
may not yet have gone so far as openly to express a judgment
on my brother. Very good, but am I summing him up to
myself unfavourably? Do I secretly pity him because he does
not see as I see? Do I despise him in my heart as weak or
eccentric? If so I am in rare peril, for my next step is to assume

I am therefore better than he. If I despise him, then it is quite certain I think over much of myself. Let me beware of classing myself as spiritually strong, for that is only to betray to God my own carnality. Of course He would have me discern clearly between right and wrong, but I must never make others the victims of my discernment. The judgment seat is Christ's, and is still future. Who of us dare usurp its function now?

OCTOBER 19th

If because of meat thy brother is grieved, thou walkest no longer in love. Romans 14. 15.

In teaching others by example, no less than by argument, it is possible to be over-bold. Here for instance is a brother whose conscience does not allow him to eat meat. So what do I do? I sit down in his presence and eat as much meat as possible, in the vain belief that by so doing I shall show him what Christian liberty is! I do not argue with him, but I put meat here and I put meat there, all in order to demonstrate to him the nature of liberty in Christ. Am I helping him, or am I "destroying" him? For note how this verse continues. It does not say "Destroy not with your argument", but "Destroy not with your meat". So if my brother and I see differently about such a matter, I should keep that difference well in the background and not thrust it on his consciousness. God commands me to do nothing to hurt him. Why? Because this is the man for whom Christ died.

OCTOBER 20th

*The firm foundation of God standeth, having this seal, the
Lord knoweth them that are his.* 2 Timothy 2. 19.

Men may go; Phygelus and Hermogenes, Hy-
menaeus and Philetus, yes, all Asia too, may prove unfaithful to
the Lord; and when they do we begin to look around and
wonder who is to be counted upon. In an hour when many
are losing their faith and lowering their standards, it is easy to
become confused. If the faith of God's children can so change,
we ask, is there anything that cannot? But think again: have
we not all of us at some time failed the Lord? Let us beware of
thinking we know human nature. Only God has that knowledge. What does the Spirit say here? The Lord knoweth
them that are His. We may be mistaken; God never is. Men
may disappoint; He cannot. And there is this also that is firm
and unchanging: *the Lord knows.*

OCTOBER 21st

Glorify God therefore in your body. 1 Corinthians 6. 20.

Hundreds of tents made up the camp of Israel, but
there was one tent quite different from all the rest. In the
common tents you could do just as you pleased: eat or fast,
work or rest, be joyful or sober, noisy or silent. But that other
tent commanded reverence and awe. As you neared it you
instinctively walked more quietly, and when you stood right
before it you bowed your head in solemn silence. What was
so very special about it? Outwardly it was of very ordinary
material; but within was the Shekinah of the living God.

"Know ye not that your body is a temple of the Holy Ghost?" Has the solemn fact dawned on us that, at new birth, very God made our hearts His dwelling-place?

OCTOBER 22nd

The twelve gates were twelve pearls; each one of the several gates was of one pearl. Revelation 21. 21.

Pearls, unlike other jewels, are drawn from the animate creation. They are produced by life—a life which has reacted to and overcome the working of death. It is when the oyster is wounded that secretly, in the depths, it produces its pearl. It was through the wounding of Jesus for our transgressions that His life was released to us His members. By divine miracle "a glorious Church" was thereby brought into being, bearing throughout, in faultless integrity, the moral character of Christ. And Matthew 13 suggests to us how infinitely precious to the Father is that most goodly pearl.

OCTOBER 23rd

The Lord's messenger in the Lord's message. Haggai 1. 13.

To His servants God gives the gift of prophecy; to the Church He gives prophets. And a prophet is one who has a history with God, one who has experienced in his own life the formative work of the Holy Spirit. We are sometimes asked by would-be preachers how many days should be spent in preparation of a sermon. The answer is at least ten years, and probably nearer twenty! In this matter at least, the proverb is usually true that "the old is better". For the preacher matters to God at least as much as the thing preached. God chooses as His prophets those in whom He has already worked out in life the thing He intends to use as His message for today.

OCTOBER 24th

Whosoever liveth and believeth on me shall never die.
John 11. 26.

Jesus came to give men life. Look through John's writings with this thought in mind. Whosoever believes may in Him have eternal life. He is the water of life and the bread of life, come to give us life "more abundantly". Moreover, because He was first willing to die, He is also to us the resurrection and the life.

In a time of crisis and calamity it is life you cling to, because it is life that matters above all else. In the Japanese air-raids on Nanking the death and destruction seemed appalling. Where before had stood pleasant homes, now all at once there were only heaps of rubble. "Is anyone in them?" was the question in every mind. Suddenly one heap began to move. A beam was thrown aside, and a man scrambled out shaking off dust and broken tiles. He could do it, because he had life!

It is by the life of Jesus that we live, a life that has been tested by death. "I am the living one . . . I have the keys of death and Hades," He proclaims. It is safest to trust in a God who raises the dead.

OCTOBER 25th

There was nothing in the ark save the two tables which Moses put there at Horeb. 2 Chronicles 5. 10.

The law written on the two stone tablets would have been a perpetual testimony against God's people. Impotent as they were to meet its demands, they would have felt only its condemnation and judgment (compare 1 Samuel 6. 19) had those tablets not been secreted within the ark. We readily agree that this ark, with its gold and acacia wood, typifies Christ our Saviour. But not merely does He stand between us and the judgment of God; He came "to fulfil" the law for us in His person, so that what was on the tablets against us has now become what is in the Ark for us. That is why the Ark of Testimony is also the Ark of the Covenant. "One jot or one tittle shall in no wise pass away from the law, till all things be accomplished."

OCTOBER 26th

O my Father, if it be possible, let this cup pass away from me. Matthew 26. 39.

Since it was to do the will of God He came, we may feel it strange that the Lord Jesus should have prayed this prayer. Yet it brings to light an important distinction. Evidently it was possible for Him to pray that the cup might be removed from Him, while it was certainly unthinkable that He should ask to be excused from doing the Father's will. The cup is, so to say, secondary to that will. It represents the thing through which the divine will finds expression—in this case the death of the cross. The Lord Jesus was wholly taken up, not with His passion as such, but with the design it fulfilled. He drank the cup because it was His Father's will, not because it was the cup.

For Jesus "the cup" was something He shrank from; for us it more often represents something we would hold on to. Our great danger may be to hold dogmatically to some "thing" associated with the divine plan for us. Every cup, however divinely appointed, should be held to very loosely. It is not that which claims us supremely, but the present will of our Father.

OCTOBER 27th

I delight to do thy will, O my God. Psalm 40. 8.

There was one occasion when I knew without doubt God had called me to a certain task. But I had lately been ill, and was as yet too weak to undertake it. So I asked God for strength. It must, I thought, be His wish to give it to me; then I would do His will. I prayed and prayed about the matter, while three months went by. Then God seemed to say: "You have asked enough. Now drop it!" I remember I was walking along the beach with a stick at the time. Coming to a halt, I drove my stick right into the sand until it was covered, stood upon it, and proclaimed: "I have dropped here the matter of my physical need." I walked on, but had scarcely gone any distance when the reality of my continuing weakness thrust itself upon me again. *Surely*, I thought, God's purpose must be realized through a renewal of my strength, and involuntarily I began to pray once more. But I checked myself. Was I not pulling His will down to the level of my own need? Walking back to the place where my stick was buried, I pointed to it. "Lord," I said, "this is my witness that I dropped the matter here, and I refuse to take it up again. Weak or strong, I am going to do Thy will." From that day, when I abandoned my personal problem and set myself to His task, my physical need began most wonderfully to be met.

OCTOBER 28th

I beseech you therefore, brethren, by the mercies of God, to present your bodies a living sacrifice, holy, acceptable to God, which is your reasonable service. Romans 12. 1.

These words take us beyond the merely individual for they imply contribution to a whole. The "presenting" is individual but the service is corporate. There are many bodies brought to Him, but the outcome is one living sacrifice. All intelligent or reasonable service to God is like this. It is essentially one service, in which nevertheless we are each to have our personal part. None may feel that what he brings is worthless to God, for it is not counted as one more or less among many separate sacrifices. Each life yielded to Him is required, so that together they may constitute that one complete whole which, we are assured, is acceptable to God. And if God is satisfied, shall not we be?

OCTOBER 29th

That they may all be one; even as thou, Father, art in me, and I in thee, that they also may be one in us: that the world may believe that thou didst send me. John 17. 21.

It is "through the Church" that the wisdom of God is manifested to spiritual powers. It is "together" that we become a habitation of God through the Spirit. Because God's children today do not function together as the Body, they have become as a leaking vessel. Shatter a glass tumbler and what happens? Each piece may perhaps hold a little water, but it is as nothing compared with what the unbroken tumbler held. So it is in spiritual things. The individual receives in but two dimensions, as it were; the Church in three. Ten thousand Christians are one thing; ten thousand members of Christ are quite another. From His fulness the Head has much more to give; but to contain it we must return to the one vessel, the one Body.

OCTOBER 30th

But I say unto you, Love your enemies. Matthew 5. 44.

I knew one man who hated another. The other man had deeply sinned against him, and so great was the injury that to have killed him would have seemed scant revenge. The one sinned against came to know the Lord, and for years saw nothing of the other man. Then, visiting a certain town, he went on Sunday to join the local believers for the Communion service. Just after he was introduced, he suddenly saw in the meeting his former enemy. He said to himself, "He is here! I did not know he was saved. What shall I do?" During the next prayer he got up quietly and went out. He began to walk away and as he walked he thought on the one hand of his salvation and on the other hand of his grievance against this man. The further away he got the worse he felt at having left the meeting and on the other hand the more incensed against his enemy. Then he thought back ten years to the time when he was saved and of how the Lord had forgiven him. Yet he felt he *could* not forgive his enemy. But the Spirit brought to his mind the word: "By this shall all men know that ye are my disciples, if ye have love one to another." He stopped short. "Lord, I forgive him!" he cried, and turning, went back to the meeting with tears streaming down his face. When he arrived they were just about to break the bread, so he arose and confessed it all, telling them how God had removed the hatred from his heart.

OCTOBER 31st

God is light, and in him is no darkness at all. 1 John 1. 5.

Whereas in John's Gospel our Lord Jesus is revealed among men as grace and truth, here in his Epistles the same Lord is discovered in existence with the Father as light and love. What was truth in the Gospel is light in the Epistles; what was grace in the Gospel is love in the Epistles. Why is this? Because light in God, when brought to men, becomes truth; love in God, when brought to men, becomes grace. Truth and grace are here, light and love back there in God. That is why it is always possible for grace to be misused, truth mishandled. Men have misappropriated these things to them-selves. But God is light and God is love, and you cannot climb

up there and touch that. It is beyond mishandling. So to recover what is lost, John does not offer us anything novel. He
takes us back to the throne and confronts us again with the
Original. For it is by returning to their source that we re-
discover first things.

NOVEMBER 1st

*Sarah said, God hath prepared laughter for me; every one
that heareth will laugh with me.* Genesis 21. 6 mg.

God had displayed complete mastery of the impossible, and Sarah's was the laugh of grateful amazement.
Earlier it had been Abraham who laughed (17. 17). But his
was the laugh of incredulity—not, be it said, directed at God,
before whom he was fallen low in obeisance, but surely at
himself. There was no disrespect; just a sense of the utter im-
possibility of it all.

Where was his faith of past years? True faith it had been, but
mingled perhaps with a certain practical "realism", a touch of
justifiable self-reliance. It was faith, so to say, in God-plus-
Abraham. Now at length he knew that the "Abraham" contribution was at an end. Only God was left to believe in. But
just here, that belief took on its new character; for favourable
conditions do not help faith, they more often hinder it. It
seems that when conditions are easy, faith is difficult; when
they are more difficult faith becomes easier; and when once
they are downright impossible, the faith of stark desperation,
having God alone to cling to, at last gives promise of that
eventual laugh of amazement.

NOVEMBER 2nd

The grace of the Lord Jesus Christ, and the love of God,
and the communion of the Holy Spirit, be with you all.
2 Corinthians 13. 14.

Love, in the heart of God, is the source of all spiritual
blessing; grace expressed in Jesus Christ has made that blessing
available to us; and communion, the coming alongside of the
Holy Spirit, is the means whereby it becomes ours. What the
Father's heart devised concerning us the Son has accomplished
for us, and now the Holy Spirit communicates it to us. When
therefore we make some fresh discovery of what is ours in
Christ, let us look for its outworking to the means God has
provided. Walk in the Spirit. Maintain obedience to Him in
all things. So doing we shall open wide the door for God to
realize in us all His desire.

NOVEMBER 3rd

No wool shall come upon them, while they minister in the
gates of the inner court, and within . . . they shall not gird
themselves with anything that causeth sweat. Ezekiel
44. 17 f.

The command is surprising, but the explanation
makes sense. Those who minister in this visionary temple shall
not wear wool but linen, because in these future conditions of
service, no work that causes perspiration will be acceptable to
the Lord. What does this tell us? The symbolism takes us back,
I think, to Genesis 3 and man's fall. Because of it the curse
rested on the ground, which therefore ceased to yield fruit

without man's effort, and Adam was told: "In the sweat of thy face shalt thou eat bread."

The work of the Lord today is not like that, but partakes of the effortless character of the coming age. Or it should, for it should be marked by the blessing of God. Only when that is withheld does fleshly effort become necessary. Please bear with me when I say that spiritual work is God's work, and when God works, man does not need to expend so much effort that he perspires over it.

NOVEMBER 4th

David sought the face of the Lord. 2 Samuel 21. 1.

There are times when we put forth tremendous effort in prayers without getting any answer from God, yet how seldom do we seek to discover why! For how can we expect God to answer prayers that are out of harmony with His mind? In all our praying we must first find the key. It was this David sought to do at the time of prolonged famine this chapter describes.

He did not simply cry to God: "This famine has lasted three years. Have mercy on us now and grant us a rich harvest this year." No, He sought the face of the Lord. Had God something to say about it? To his direct question God gave a direct reply, and with it the key to answered prayer. Saul, it appears, by slaying some of the Gibeonites, had violated God's understanding with Israel to spare them. True, he had done it out of zeal for God; but he had sinned. God will not permit the breaking of a solemn vow. So there was something to be set right. "And after that," we read in verse 14, "God was intreated for the land." David had found the key.

NOVEMBER 5th

*He that cometh to God must believe that he is, and that he
is a rewarder of them that seek after him.* Hebrews 11. 6.

       Three facts about God underlie true faith: He is able
(Matthew 9. 28), He is willing (Matthew 8. 2 f.), and the fact
quoted here: He is. And mark you, by this last article of faith
I do not mean some vague belief that there is a God. I mean
the conviction that *God is*: living, present, active.

  Let us suppose you have pointed a sinner to Christ. When
you have prayed with him and he has prayed, you ask him
where he stands now. If he replies that God can save him, are
you satisfied? Even if he goes further and affirms that God will
save him, is that enough? No, you will not be content until he
has expressed the conviction that God *has* saved him, that God
is His Saviour. We shall get nowhere with "God can" and
"God will" if we stop short of "God is". For His power and
His compassion by themselves may stir us only to hope. Faith
rests on His activity now. Do not claim to have faith until you
can say, "I am . . . and I have . . . because God is!"

NOVEMBER 6th

*Put on the whole armour of God, that ye may be able to
stand against the wiles of the devil.* Ephesians 6. 11.

       Here the verb "stand" means "hold your ground".
It is not, in modern parlance, a command to march—to invade
a foreign territory in order to occupy and subdue it. God has
not told us to do this. "Stand" implies that the ground dis-
puted by the enemy is really His, and therefore ours. It was the

Lord Jesus who carried the offensive into Satan's kingdom, to gain by death and resurrection a mighty victory. Today we fight only to maintain and consolidate the victory He has gained. That is perhaps why the armour described here is largely defensive. For the territory is His. We do not fight to gain a foothold on it. We only need to hold it against all challengers.

NOVEMBER 7th

In all these things we are more than conquerors through him that loved us. Romans 8. 37.

In Christ we *are already* conquerors. Is it not obvious then, since this is so, that merely to pray for victory—unless that prayer is shot through with praise—must be to court defeat by throwing away our fundamental position? Let me ask you: Has defeat been your experience? Have you found yourself hoping that one day you will be strong enough to win? Then my prayer for you can go no further than that of the apostle Paul for his Ephesian readers. It is that God may open your eyes anew to see yourself seated with Him who has Himself been made to sit "far above all rule, and authority, and power, and dominion, and every name that is named" (1. 20 f.). The difficulties around you may not alter; the lion may roar as loudly as ever; but you need no longer *hope* to overcome. In Christ Jesus you *are* victor in the field.

NOVEMBER 8th

The king's daughter within the palace is all glorious; her clothing is inwrought with gold. Psalm 45. 13.

The bride is to be led into the King's presence in a bridal dress skilfully and patiently prepared of "broidered work". There *is* a garment that is a gift outright; but the bride's attire is not merely gold, that is to say, what proceeds purely from God. It is "inwrought with gold", which surely means that gold thread is patiently woven or embroidered into the fabric itself. This suggests, does it not, the Spirit's continuous application to her experience of the realities of the cross of Calvary, in order that the glories of Christ may be displayed. Here is a divine working in which she is the willing co-operator. The Lamb's wife "hath made herself ready".

NOVEMBER 9th

The fear of the Lord is the beginning of wisdom: and the knowledge of the Holy One is understanding. Proverbs 9. 10.

Folly or wisdom? The question hinges simply on procrastination or prompt obedience. Some of us are parents and have children. How greatly those children can differ in temperament! One will obey at once; another will think that by putting it off he can avoid the need to do so. If that is indeed the case, and you are weak enough to allow him a loophole for escape, then the one who procrastinates is in fact the wise one, for he succeeds in doing nothing. But if your word holds and ultimately must be obeyed, then he is certainly the wiser who faces the issue squarely at once. Get clear about the will of God. If God's words can be discounted, then you might not be foolish to try to escape their implications; but if God is an unchanging God with an unchanging will, then be wise; act now; redeem the time.

NOVEMBER 10th

These all with one accord continued steadfastly in prayer.
Acts 1. 14.

How is God's will to be done on earth? Only by His having on his side a willing people. Only by every one of us remembering, in the solemn conditions of today, that the Church at prayer is heaven's outlet, the channel of release for heaven's power, and that this ministry is our greatest possible work. God shows what He wants, we stand and ask, and God acts from heaven: this is true prayer, and this is what we must see fully expressed in our prayer meetings. If the Church here in Shanghai, not to speak of other places, does not know this ministry of prayer, may God forgive us! Without it, all else is empty; God has no vessel here.

NOVEMBER 11th

I will run the way of thy commandments, when thou shalt enlarge my heart. Psalm 119. 32.

Many of our ills today stem from the fact that we are content with a merely objective acceptance of doctrine. We seek an outward, mental light on the Scriptures, but stop short of their inward application to experience. We encounter many intellectual difficulties in the Bible; and "light", to us, is the solving of these. For many of us it is a case of feeling all is well if we are conservative or orthodox in our doctrine, and give mental assent to this and mental dissent from that. It is by this reasoning that fundamentalists consider themselves on a so much higher plane than modernists. Yet surely it must be obvious to us that we all measure up spiritually in God's eyes only in so far as we possess a true inward knowledge of His Son, and no further. We may be perfectly right, but unless we possess His life and live by that, we lack the supreme essential.

NOVEMBER 12th

Blessed are they that wash their robes, that they may have the right to come to the tree of life. Revelation 22. 14.

It was not by committing murder that Adam let sin into the world. That came later. Adam let in sin by his free choice between these two trees: the one whose name is Life, and the one that offered him the independent power to decide for himself on moral issues. By a deliberate act he turned to the latter, choosing to have his soul developed to a place where he could go on alone apart from God. When therefore God secures for His glory a race of men who will be the instrument to accomplish His purpose in the universe, they will be a people whose life—yea, whose very breath—is dependent upon Him. He will be the "tree of life" to them.

NOVEMBER 13th

After this manner therefore pray ye: Our Father which art in heaven, Hallowed be thy name. Matthew 6. 9.

Our Father! The inter-dependence of God's people is not just a comfortable thought. It is a vital factor in their life. We cannot get on without one another. It is true that "God hath dealt to each man a measure of faith" (Romans 12. 3), but alone in isolation man can never exercise it to the full, as the context of that verse makes clear. It needs a complete Body to attain to the stature of Christ and to display His glory. That is why fellowship in prayer is so important. Trusting the Lord by myself is good, but may not be enough. I must trust Him also with others. I must learn to pray on the basis of oneness with my brethren in Christ, for only together shall we get through in prayer to God's end. I need the help of the Body because I need the help of the Lord, and because His life is the life of the Body.

NOVEMBER 14th

Jesus said, Make the people sit down. John 6. 10.

Our Christian life today is a foretaste of the heavenly banquet still to come; for God has "made us to sit down with him" who first was seated by mighty power in the heavenly places far above all (Ephesians 1. 20; 2. 6). This means that the work of salvation is not ours but His. It is not that we work for God but that He has worked for us. God *gives* us our position of rest. He brings His Son's finished work and presents it to us, and then He says to us, "Please sit" (*ch'eng tso*). His offer of salvation cannot, I think, be better expressed than in the words of invitation to the great feast in the parable: "Come; for all things are now ready."

NOVEMBER 15th

Ye shall find rest unto your souls. Matthew 11. 29.

There is a rest which is given: "I will give you rest"; but there is rest also which has to be found. The first is obtained simply by coming to God and receiving His gift of life. This means something more than just believing in a well-preached evangelical gospel. It means coming as a weary, burdened sinner and making living personal contact with the Lord Jesus Christ Himself. Such contact unfailingly brings rest. Thank God for all His children who possess this fundamental gift!

But having come there, we find ourselves on the threshhold of something more. We are to learn of Him—to discover the deep satisfaction to be found in a growing knowledge of the Lord Himself. Above all, we are to learn His meekness and lowliness of heart. In doing so, He says, we shall find rest. For this rest is not a gift; it is for disciples, that is to say, learners. And learning takes time, but it is also infinitely rewarding.

*Take my yoke upon you and learn of me; for I am meek
and lowly in heart.* Matthew 11. 29.

What is it to be yoked to the Lord? It implies willing,
contented cooperation with Him in the divine plan. Of course
the yoke limits the ox; it cannot wander all over the field as it
pleases, but must take a straight line forward. That way the
work gets done however. And here is the value of the lowliness of heart that does not think big, ambitious things of itself,
but is willing for any place God appoints, even though it be at
the very bottom.

In this chapter of Matthew we see the apparent frustration of
the Lord's public ministry, in that only babes had understood
and responded to it. "How undignified!" we might exclaim.
But no: "I thank thee, O Father," were His words, "for so it
was well-pleasing in thy sight." He is not aiming at anything.
He is perfectly willing for what God has ordained. And the
question is, Are we content to accept His limitations and go
along with Him? For the deepest rest is this "rest unto our
souls".

NOVEMBER 17th

*I was with you in weakness, and in fear, and in much
trembling, . . . but in demonstration of the Spirit and of
power.* 1 Corinthians 2. 3 f.

Scripture presents to us two kinds of Christian experience, both equally valid and necessary. On the one hand
there are such strong, almost boastful affirmations as: "God
. . . always leadeth us in triumph in Christ", "To me to live is

Christ" and "I can do all things in him that strengtheneth me".
Yet on the other hand the very same people, with equal truth,
have to confess: "We despaired even of life", "Christ Jesus
came into the world to save sinners; of whom I am chief", and
"We also are weak in him". This latter seems to be another
kind of Christian, faulty, frail and fearful, and alarmingly
lacking in confidence. But in fact the real life of a child of God
consists in the co-existence of these two experiences. We
would prefer of course to concentrate on the first only, to the
exclusion of the other. But to know them both is to know
Him who is the God of Israel—and the God of Jacob too!

NOVEMBER 18th

Only rebel not against the Lord, neither fear ye the people
of the land: for they are bread for us. Numbers 14. 9.

The trials confronting us on the way to full enjoyment of our inheritance in Christ may be quite as gigantic as
were some of the Canaanites, but God intends to use them for
our increase. Faith sees them as its food. If we but knew it, we
thrive and grow on difficulties. But the reverse is also true.
The ten spies reported in dismay that Canaan was "a land
which eateth up the inhabitants thereof" (13. 32). Abandon
your faith in God and turn away from the problem and you
put yourself in a position to be swallowed up by what was
meant for your growth. Many of us dodge difficulties. We
walk round the issue seeking an easy way out. We shelve the
question instead of confronting it squarely. We will not face
what is involved in that hazardous Jordan crossing and the
terrors we apprehend just beyond. Oh yes, we escape the
trials; but we starve!

Food is our life, but we cannot get it by a spiritual holiday. Let us miss no opportunity to prove the Lord. The foe may trouble us, but that way lies nourishment and spiritual enlargement.

NOVEMBER 19th

When the vessel that he made of the clay was marred in the hand of the potter, he made it again another vessel, as seemed good to the potter to make it. Jeremiah 18. 4.

The Potter's original design became marred by something unresponsive in the clay. Yes marred, but not destroyed, for He made it again another vessel. It is wonderful what God can still do, provided always we are prepared for His adjustments. Have we failed Him somewhere? Then it were folly to persist in what He has abandoned, falsely imagining He is compelled to go on with us in it.

Has He perchance changed His mind? Am I now ordained to be "another vessel"? If so it were death to strive to be the former one. "Cannot I do with you as this potter?" says the Lord. We cannot play with His will. Though our loving Father, He is nevertheless sovereign in His ways. Our attitude should be: "Keep me near Thee, fearing Thee, always ready for Thy best!" I find great personal comfort in the counsel of Peter: "Humble yourselves therefore under the mighty hand of God, that he may exalt you in due time" (1 Peter 5. 6).

NOVEMBER 20th

Master, we toiled all night, and took nothing. Luke 5. 5.

There are times when the efforts expended in the work of the Lord warrant our looking for certain results, but to our dismay they do not appear. "Why this vain toil?" we ask ourselves. "To think it could be possible for us to toil all night and to go unblessed!" But it is useless to argue here. The fact has simply to be faced that God has withheld His blessing. In human affairs we reason from cause to effect, but all our reasonings are irrelevant in the realm of divine favour. In that realm God is the Cause, and He alone.

"But at thy word I will let down the nets": this is the kind of faith that avails in His service. It trusts Him to bless us beyond all our deserts. Provided our expectation is in Him alone, I believe we shall see blessing on all our future way. The favour of the Lord resting on one life may mean the salvation of fifty lives; it may mean the consecration to Him of a hundred lives. God's blessing has momentous results. Let us expect the supernatural. Let us look to God for miracles.

NOVEMBER 21st

I know whom I have believed. 2 Timothy 1. 12.

If you ask a number of believers who have entered upon the fulness of life in Christ how they came by their experience, some will say in this way and some will say in that. Each stresses his own particular mode of entering in and produces Scripture to support his experience; and unhappily many Christians are using their special experiences and special Scriptures to fight other Christians. The fact of the matter is that, while Christians may enter into this fuller life by different ways, provided Christ is their centre, we need not regard their experiences or doctrines as mutually exclusive, but rather complementary. For one thing is certain: any experience of value in the sight of God must have been reached by way of a new discovery of the meaning of the person and work of the Lord Jesus. There is no other way. This is a safe test and a crucial one.

NOVEMBER 22nd

Faith is the substantiating of things hoped for. Hebrews 11. 1 (J. N. Darby Trans.).

How do we "substantiate" something? We are doing it every day. We cannot live in the world without doing it. A "substance" is an object, something before me, though it may be no more tangible than sound or colour. "Substantiating" means that I have a certain faculty of hearing or sight that makes that intangible "substance" real to me. For instance, the colour yellow is quite real; but if I shut my eyes, then to me it has lost its reality; it is simply nothing—*to me*. With my faculty of sight to substantiate it, however, yellow becomes yellow to me. Not only is the colour there; I have given it reality in my consciousness. How precious is the gift of sight!

But even more than music or colour, the "hoped for" things of Christ are eternal and therefore real; and I have been given one precious faculty that can substantiate them. Faith, the faith of the Son of God, is this faculty. It makes divine things to become real in my experience. By resting on God's faithfulness, faith substantiates *to me* the unseen things I as yet barely hope for.

NOVEMBER 23rd

He saith unto me, See thou do it not: I am a fellow-servant
with thee . . . Worship God. Revelation 19. 10.

What had happened? Had John lost his head, that he should try to worship an angel? Well, he may have lost his head, but what is quite certain is that he had been carried away in his heart. There are those who have such good heads, they never do stupid things. John was not of that number, for twice he repeated this blunder (cf. 22. 8). The truth is he had a good heart, and good hearts may sometimes become confused and do stupid things. His heart was overwhelmed with wonder at this glorious Church "coming down out of heaven from God", and at the amazing fact that, in his own patience and tribulation, he was sharing with heavenly labourers in this the greatest divine masterpiece of all time. His act was wrong, no doubt, but it sprang from a right attitude, and one we might safely emulate.

NOVEMBER 24th

A new covenant: not of the letter, but of the spirit: for the
letter killeth, but the spirit giveth life. 2 Corinthians 3. 6.

It is wearisome to me, if not actually repulsive, to talk with folk who aim at perfect outward correctness, while caring little for what is vital and spiritual. "Missionary methods", as such, do not interest me at all. In fact, it is a deep grief to meet children of God who know practically nothing of the hatefulness of a life lived in the energy of the natural man, and have little vital experience of the headship of Jesus Christ, yet who all the while are scrupulously careful to arrive at absolute correctness of method in God's service. God Himself has provided for His wine the wine-skin which will best contain and mature it. It is loss, certainly, to have wine without a wine-skin, but it is worse than loss, it is death, to have a wine-skin without wine.

NOVEMBER 25th

Our old man was crucified with him . . . that so we should no longer be in bondage to sin. Romans 6. 6.

Why do you believe that the Lord Jesus died? What is your ground for that belief? Is it that you feel He has died? No, you have never felt it. You believe it because the Word of God tells you so. When the Lord was crucified, two thieves were crucified at the same time. You do not doubt that they were crucified with Him, either, because the Scripture says so quite plainly. Now, what about your own death? Your crucifixion with Christ is more intimate than theirs. They were crucified at the same time as the Lord, but on different crosses, whereas you were crucified on the self-same cross as He, for you were in Him when He died. It does not depend on your feelings. You can know it is so for the one sufficient reason that God has said it is so. That Christ has died is a fact, that the two thieves have died is a fact, and that you have died is a fact also. The self you loathe is on the cross in Christ! And "he that is dead is freed from sin"!

NOVEMBER 26th

Why stand ye here all the day idle? . . . Go ye also into the vineyard. Matthew 20. 6 f.

This word "idle", Greek *argos*, helps greatly to illumine Paul's doctrine of deliverance from sin, for it forms the root of the word he uses in Romans 6.6 when he writes of the body of sin being "done away", that is to say "made ineffective", "put out of operation", by the Cross. Sin, the old master, is still about, but in Christ the slave who served him has been put to death, and so is out of reach and his members are unemployed. The gambler's hand is unemployed, the swearer's tongue is unemployed, and these members are now available to be used instead as "instruments of righteousness unto God". To be able under these circumstances to say, in reply to the Lord's question, "Because no man hath hired us," is to invite employment by Him in the most rewarding service there is. "Go ye also into my vineyard, and whatsoever is right I will give you."

NOVEMBER 27th

As ye presented your members as servants to uncleanness and to iniquity unto iniquity, even so now present your members as servants to righteousness unto sanctification. Romans 6. 19.

Once a Chinese brother, travelling by train, found himself in a carriage together with three non-Christians. To while away the time these men wished to play cards, and lacking a fourth to complete the game, they invited him to join them. "I am sorry to disappoint you," he said, "but I cannot, for I have not brought my hands with me." "What ever do you mean?" they asked in blank astonishment. "This pair of hands does not belong to me," he said, and then there followed the explanation of the transfer of ownership that had taken place in his life. "Present your members," says Paul, "as instruments of righteousness unto God," and that brother regarded the members of his body therefore as belonging entirely to the Lord. This is holiness in practice.

NOVEMBER 28th

Not in wisdom of words, lest the Cross of Christ should be made void. 1 Corinthians 1. 17.

When I was younger I sought to attain to a perfect standard of presenting divine truth, determined to leave nothing that could possibly be misunderstood by the hearers. I took great care to run no risks in my preaching, but I must confess there was very little spiritual value in it. God, I soon discovered, uses the weak things as His messengers. He does not demand of us fool-proof explanations but uses fragments, a word here, a sentence there, to bring to men His flashes of light. He is not looking for perfect understanding or for faultless teaching; indeed our very desire for perfection in these matters may itself hinder Him if it stands in the way of His first object, which is to bring life to dead souls, heavenly manna to hungry hearts. "The words that I have spoken unto you are spirit, and are life."

NOVEMBER 29th

I have seen thy face, as one seeth the face of God. Genesis
33. 10.

What does this astonishing statement mean? Jacob,
who had seen God face to face at Peniel, now describes his
meeting with Esau as if he were again seeing the face of God!
It may have been mere flattery, an evidence that Jacob still
retained something of his earlier scheming nature. It may also
have been a kind of confession that all his elaborately planned
arrangement of his family and possessions had been a waste of
time. In Esau's welcome he may have recognized that deliverance had come to him, not through his own clever artifice
but through the overruling of God. But there is one more
possible meaning, and this is a universal spiritual fact. It is that
those whom we have wronged will always represent God to
us. When we meet them, it is as though we were meeting
God. It can be in judgment. Thank God if, when this is so, our
hearts are truly humbled before Him. It can also mean mercy
and reconciliation. "First be reconciled to thy brother, and
then come and offer thy gift."

NOVEMBER 30th

I have waited for thy salvation, O Lord. Genesis 49. 18.

Genesis chapter 49 reveals Jacob as a prophet. Out of
a real understanding of God's heart he could utter its tremendous forecasts. But this verse, set right in the middle, is
not a prophecy; it is a cry of Jacob himself. For there was
sorrow and a foreboding of sin as well as joy and good in these
oracles, and he had just been compelled to paint a very dark

picture of Dan as a serpent in the pathway. Then, just here, Jacob showed himself. Lifting his eyes to heaven he revealed what he, the prophet, was. It is easy enough to preach; but when a man preaches we know at once if God has hold of him or not. The old Jacob would have begun to think up a scheme for dealing with Dan. He could always get the better of people; but not now. Now he had learned to know God. "I have waited for thy salvation, O Lord!"

DECEMBER 1st

Out of much affliction and anguish of heart I wrote unto you . . . that ye might know the love which I have more abundantly unto you. 2 Corinthians 2. 4.

A ministry that is to bring healing and life must spring essentially from experience. This fact is strikingly displayed in the apostle Paul. The ministry of 1 Corinthians, for example, is based firmly on the man revealed to us in 2 Corinthians.

In 1 Corinthians Paul writes of God's choice of "the weak things"; 2 Corinthians shows in grim reality his own experience of a divinely imposed weakness. In the first letter Paul appeals to his readers for unity; in the second he shows how, in spite of their rebuffs, he still counts himself one of them. Chapter 13 of the first letter offers his classic treatment of love; in 2 Corinthians 12. 15 he affirms, "I will most gladly spend and be spent for your souls." Finally, 1 Corinthians 15 gives us the clearest teaching anywhere in the New Testament on the subject of the resurrection; yet 2 Corinthians makes plain his own desperate need to trust from hour to hour in "God which raiseth the dead". At every point his doctrine is backed with experience. Nothing else really constitutes a basis for a ministry of Christ.

DECEMBER 2nd

Wherewithal shall a young man cleanse his way? By taking heed thereto according to thy word. Psalm 119. 9.

The Pharisees cleansed the outside of the platter, but left the inside full of impurity. Our Lord rebuked them for setting so much store on outward things and ignoring the inward, and many of us conclude from this that, provided we stress the inwardness of spiritual truth, all is well. But God demands both inward and outward purity. To have the outer without the inner is spiritual death, but to have the inner without the outer is only spiritualized life. For to by-pass things by spiritualizing them is not spirituality. "These things ye ought to have done, and not to have left the other undone" (Matthew 23. 23). No matter how trifling a divine command may seem, it is an expression of the will of God. Never dare we treat it lightly. We cannot with impunity neglect even the least of His wishes.

DECEMBER 3rd

Apart from me ye can do nothing. John 15. 5.

The temptation to try is ingrained in human nature. Let me tell you something I have seen in my own country at the salt pits. In China some coolies can carry a load of salt weighing 120 kilos; others as much as 250 kilos. Now along comes a man who can only carry 120 kilos, and here is a load of 250 kilos. He knows perfectly well it is far too heavy for him, but although he cannot possibly carry it he still tries.

As a youngster I used to amuse myself watching ten or twenty of these fellows come along and try, though every one of them knew he could not possibly manage it. In the end he must give up and make way for the man who could. How often is it only at the point of utter despair with ourselves that we remember the Lord and relinquish to Him the task He is so ready and able to perform! The sooner we do so the better, for while we monopolize it we leave little room for the Spirit's mighty working.

DECEMBER 4th

Christ Jesus, who was made unto us wisdom from God, and righteousness and sanctification, and redemption. 1 Corinthians 1. 30.

God has given us Christ. There is nothing now for us to receive outside of Him. The Holy Spirit has been sent to produce what is of Christ in us; not to produce anything that is apart from or outside of Him. *He* "was made unto us . . .". This is one of the grandest statements in Scripture. If we believe this, we can put in there anything we need, and can know that God has made it good; for, through the Holy Spirit within us, the Lord Jesus is Himself made unto us whatever we lack. We have been accustomed to look upon holiness as a virtue, upon humility as a grace, upon love as a gift to be sought from God. But the Christ of God is *Himself* everything that we shall ever need. Let us unhesitatingly draw upon Him.

DECEMBER 5th

They cast therefore, and now they were not able to draw it for the multitude of fishes. That disciple therefore whom Jesus loved saith unto Peter, It is the Lord. John 21. 6 f.

As Jesus stood there on the shore, the strange thing was that none of them knew Him; not even Peter and John who had been most intimate with Him, nor Thomas who so lately had identified Him by His wounds. The risen Lord was not to be recognized merely by human eyes, nor by hands of flesh. Even when He spoke to them of familiar things, still they did not recognize Him. But when the net was full, John suddenly knew.

Later, when on shore Jesus said "Come and break your fast," none of them, we are told, dared ask Him "Who art thou?" knowing it was the Lord. Here is a paradox. In the ordinary way, if you ask a question it implies a lack of knowledge; if you dare not ask, it suggests a fear of displaying that lack. But here we have both fear and knowledge. With the outward man they feared, but with the inward man they knew. Often you cannot explain, yet there is an inward, divinely given assurance. This is Christianity.

DECEMBER 6th

I can do all things in him that strengtheneth me. Philippians 4. 13.

In the work of God today things are often so constituted that we have no need to rely upon God. But the Lord's verdict upon all such work is uncompromising: "Apart from me ye can do nothing." For divine work can only be done with divine power, and that power is to be found only in the Lord Jesus. It is when we reach the point of saying with the prophet, "I cannot speak," that we discover God is speaking. He never asks us to do anything we can do. He asks us to live a life we can never live and to do a work we can never do. Yet by His grace we are living it and doing it. The life we live is the life of Christ lived in the power of God, and the work we do is the work of Christ carried on through us by His Spirit whom we obey.

DECEMBER 7th

He looked upon Jesus as he walked, and saith, Behold the Lamb of God! John 1. 36.

When John first announced Christ as the Lamb of God, he added: "which taketh away the sin of the world" (verse 29), thus emphasizing His redeeming work. The second time he did so, however, he simply said: "Behold the Lamb of God!" Here the accent was not so much on the work as on the Person. Real appreciation means that people are precious to us for their own sakes. We come to love them more for what they are than for what they have done. So it should be with our appreciation of Christ. We thank the Lord for His gifts, but we praise Him for His worth. Christ on the Cross calls forth from us our amazed thanksgiving; Christ on the throne our praise. We behold what He has done and we are profoundly grateful; we behold who He is and we adore.

DECEMBER 8th

Blessed is he, whosoever shall not be offended in me. Luke
7. 23. A.V.

John the Baptist did not like it. He had looked for a
new revival such as the first Elijah had witnessed, and here he
lay in prison with death imminent. If he himself must achieve
nothing, surely Jesus ought to take some action to vindicate
this second Elijah ministry.

Are we offended when God does not do what we feel he
should? We have sought to know His will and want only His
glory, and yet many of His ways we find disappointing. We
have met some impasse and found no way through; we were
ill and expected Him to heal us and we were not healed; we
are short of money and money does not come. Or far worse,
it is some matter in which God's very honour seems at stake.
He *must* come in for the sake of His name—and yet He does
not. The situation is unchanged, no prison gates open, no
hearts melt, none cry "Sirs, what must I do?"

There is a day when all will be explained. When we stand
before the judgment seat, not only shall we be judged; God
will explain things to us. In much we shall be proved wrong,
but there will be many things of which He will say: "I was
right, but you were right also."

DECEMBER 9th

Ye also ought to wash one another's feet. John 13. 14.

The washing alluded to here is for refreshment; it
does not relate to sin. Unlike sin, the dust and dirt that gather
on our feet are inevitable. To roll in the dust would be sin,

certainly, but if we touch the earth at all our feet will be dusty. A brother working long hours in an office comes back home at the end of the day, tired and out of tune with things. He finds it difficult to recover the refreshment of communion with his Lord he had in his morning quiet time. There is a coating of something upon him which makes him unable to rise up to the Lord at once.

But a friend meets him and quite spontaneously praises the Lord. At once he feels a lifting power. It is as though someone had taken a duster and wiped the film away. His feet are clean once more. To "wash one another's feet" is to return things to their former freshness in this way. It is possible to be largely unaware of the fact that we are doing it, and yet to be constantly used thus to refresh our brethren in Christ. I tell you, it is one of the greatest ministries.

DECEMBER 10th

He smote thrice, and stayed. And the man of God was wroth with him, and said, Thou shouldest have smitten five or six times. 2 Kings 13. 18 f.

We are always in danger of setting a limit to what God can do. Today God wants us to prepare for a new release in the work of the Gospel, but we set Him a target beyond which our faith is not prepared to go. We have not understood the flight of the Lord's "arrow of victory". Our gratification over the hundred souls that have come to Him may be the thing that hinders them coming in their thousands. Is it not possible that the large hall we have built for the proclamation of the Gospel may impose a limit on future growth? There is always a grave danger of circumscribing God's grace. The blessing He gives is intended to pave the way for greater blessing, never to become a barrier to it. By all means let us work to a plan, but let us shake ourselves free from all trammels of the past and live in a state of constant expectancy. Right ahead of us lies a work immensely greater than that which lies behind. God plans for us unprecedented blessings.

DECEMBER 11th

By grace have ye been saved through faith; and that not of yourselves: it is the gift of God. Ephesians 2. 8.

We rightly speak of being saved through faith, but what do we mean by it? We mean this, that we are saved by reposing in the Lord Jesus. We did nothing whatever to save ourselves; we simply laid upon Him the burden of our sin-sick souls. We began our Christian life by depending not upon our own doing but upon what He had done. Until a man does this he is no Christian; for to say, "I can do nothing to save myself, but by His grace God has done everything for me in Christ," is to take the first step in the life of faith. There is no limit to the grace God is willing to bestow upon us.

DECEMBER 12th

He is not ashamed to call them brethren. Hebrews 2. 11.

In the outset of the Fourth Gospel the Evangelist describes Jesus as "the only begotten from the Father". At the end of the same book the risen Lord says to Mary Magdalene, "Go unto my brethren, and say to them, I ascend unto my Father and your Father" (John 20. 17). Hitherto in this Gospel

Jesus had spoken of "the Father" or of "my Father". Now in resurrection He adds: ". . . and your Father". How wonderful this is, for it is the eldest Son now, "the first begotten from the dead," who is speaking. By His incarnation and Cross He has added many sons to God's family, and so in the same verse He speaks of them as "my brethren". And praise God, by His exaltation you and I have received the spirit of adoption whereby now we too cry, Abba, Father. "The Spirit himself beareth witness with our spirit, that we are children of God."

DECEMBER 13th

Nay, much rather, those members of the body which seem to be more feeble are necessary. 1 Corinthians 12. 22.

Once, years ago, I was faced with a very big problem in my life, and one to which I knew I could not find the solution alone. I was preaching the Gospel at the time in a remote region, far from other servants of God with anything approaching the knowledge of His Word that I felt was essential to help me discover the answer. Where was I to find the fellowship I needed? There were of course the few believers, country folk, among whom I was staying, but they were mere babes in Christ. How could they possibly help solve *this* problem?

However, I had reached an impasse. There was indeed nothing left but to call them in; so at my request those simple brothers came to me in my need. I told them what I could of my difficulty, and they prayed—and as they prayed, light dawned! The thing did not need explaining. It was done, and done in such a way as never to need repeating. How our God delights to display to us our dependence on His "feeble members"!

DECEMBER 14th

Not forsaking the assembling of ourselves together, as the custom of some is, but exhorting one another; and so much the more as ye see the day drawing nigh. Hebrews 10. 25.

Christ is the Head of the Church and "we, who are many, are one body in Christ, and severally members one of another". All Christian relationships therefore are of one member to another, never of a head to the members. When an apostle is preaching a grand sermon, and all the believers are nodding assent and adding their frequent and fervent "Amens", how deeply spiritual the congregation seems! But it is when they meet by themselves that their true spiritual state comes to light. The "pulpit-and-pew" principle, so vital for proclaiming the glad tidings to sinners, nevertheless tends to foster passivity in Christian life. It is by the "round table" principle of mutuality, by believers exhorting one another, that the Church lives and grows. Has our fellowship together the true stamp of "one another" upon it?

DECEMBER 15th

It is God . . . who shined in our hearts, to give the light of the knowledge of the glory of God in the face of Jesus Christ. 2 Corinthians 4. 6.

What is salvation? It is the breaking in of divine light. The veiling of that light meant perdition. But God has shined into the hearts of us who were perishing; and merely to *see* is salvation. As soon as we see the glory in the Saviour's face, in that instant we are saved. If we merely understand the doctrine and assent to it, nothing happens, for we have not *seen* Him who is the Truth. But as surely as the impression on a film follows the opening of the camera shutter, so the moment we really see Him as Saviour, in that moment the inward transformation begins, and what was to us "the heavenly vision" becomes in turn "His Son revealed *in me*" (Acts 26. 19; Galatians 1. 16). There is no need to remind ourselves of such a living experience. You can never forget it.

DECEMBER 16th

There is yet one man by whom we may inquire of the Lord, Micaiah the son of Imlah: but I hate him. 1 Kings 22. 8.

Obsession is a terrible thing. To lie is to deceive others, knowing one is lying. To be obsessed is to have deceived oneself; to lie, and not know it; to have moved beyond reach of conscience to the point where the light that is in us is darkness. It is, in short, to have shut out the truth. This state is reached by the simple choice of darkness. "Every one that doeth ill hateth the light, and cometh not to the light." "And for this cause God sendeth them a working of error, that they should believe a lie" (John 3. 19 ff.; 2 Thessalonians 2. 11). So in the end the obsessed are true; they have come to believe in what they are doing! Saul of Tarsus "verily thought . . .".

How are we delivered? By one thing only: light. "He that doeth the truth cometh to the light." God need do no further work. I am sometimes asked: "Why always speak of revelation? Why not emphasize God's work of deliverance?" I reply: Because the revelation *is* the work. By it Saul knew himself a blasphemer. By it Job was moved to say: "Now mine eye seeth thee, wherefore I abhor myself and repent." There is no second work. God makes us *see*, and that is enough.

DECEMBER 17th

O thou afflicted, tossed with the tempest, and not com-
forted, behold I will set thy stones in fair colours, and lay
thy foundations with sapphires. Isaiah 54. 11.

Along with the gold in both Eden and Paradise we
find precious stones (Genesis 2. 12; Revelation 21. 19). Gem-
stones are not produced in a day. Time is a vital factor in their
formation. They are wrought by long process in the fires of
earth, and their beauties are displayed by skilful cutting. In
spiritual terms this implies values that are inwardly wrought
by the divine patience in you and me. Such values are costly.
Those unwilling to pay will never come by them. Grace is
free; but only a high price buys precious stones. Many a time
we shall want to cry out, "This is costing too much!" Yet the
lessons we learn as we pass with Him "through fire and
water"—these are the really worth-while things. In the light
of God some things perish of themselves; there is no need to
wait for the fire. It is in what has stood God's test of time that
true worth lies.

DECEMBER 18th

In the name of Jesus Christ of Nazareth, walk. Acts 3. 6.

Consider these words of Peter to the crippled man
at the gate: *In the Name.* Clearly no other name, least of all his
own, would have brought the same dramatic result. Let me
give you a simple illustration. Some time ago my fellow-
worker sent to me for a sum of money. I read his letter, prepared what he had asked, and gave the sum to the messenger.
Was I right? Yes, certainly. The letter bore my friend's

signature, and to me that was enough. Should I instead have asked the messenger his name and age and employment and native place, and then perhaps sent him away because I objected to what he was? No, by no means, for he had come in my friend's name, and I honoured that name.

God looks at His Son in the glory; not at us here on the earth, and He honours His Son's Name. All that took place that day resulted from the impact of the Name of Jesus on the situation, and the only thing that distinguished His servants was that they were authorized to use that Name.

DECEMBER 19th

Lest any root of bitterness springing up trouble you, and thereby the many be defiled. Hebrews 12. 15.

The favour of the Lord may be likened to a wild bird that you are seeking to lure into a room. Try as you may, you cannot induce it to fly in. It must do so of its own accord; and then, if it does, you will have to be on the alert lest it fly out again. You could not persuade it to enter, but you can easily cause it to depart. Just a little carelessness on your part, and it is gone!

In blessing us, it is God who takes the initiative; no effort is called for on our side. But when His blessing has been fully bestowed, it takes but a little heedlessness on our part to lose it. The divine favour is to be found where brethren are living in harmony; never, as we well know, where there is discord among them. Do you realize how serious a thing it is to be at variance with any brother, even if a consideration of every aspect of the case proves you to be right? At all costs give heed to your words, lest you forfeit the Lord's favour, and awake to find the bird flown!

DECEMBER 20th

Even so ye also, when ye shall have done all the things that are commanded you, say, We are unprofitable servants; we have done that which it was our duty to do. Luke 17. 10.

Two kinds of work may occupy the servant in this passage: "ploughing" or "keeping sheep", both very important occupations. Yet even when he returns from such work, Jesus reminds us that he is expected to provide for his master's satisfaction before sitting down to enjoy his own meal. When we return from our toil in the field, be it preaching the Gospel to the unsaved or tending the needs of the flock, we are apt to muse complacently on the much work we have accomplished! But the Lord will say to us: "Gird thyself and serve Me." Of course we ourselves must eat and drink, but not till His thirst is quenched, His hunger satisfied. We too shall have our enjoyment, but that can never be until His joy is full. Let us ask ourselves often: Does our work for Him minister first of all to our satisfaction, or to His?

DECEMBER 21st

They shall not teach every man his fellow-citizen, and every man his brother, saying, Know the Lord: for all shall know me from the least to the greatest of them. Hebrews 8. 11.

In seeking to know God's will under the old covenant, men were, generally speaking, restricted to the law and the prophets. But Christianity is based not on information but on revelation. Do you have a book-knowledge of Christ? Do you know Him only by hearsay, so to speak, from some true servant of His? Or are you in direct touch with your Lord? It is one of the most precious factors in our Christian life to have friends who live close to God and who can share with us what He has shown them. Again and again we need their arresting challenge or the calm of their mature counsel. But the New Covenant affirms that "All shall know me", and the word translated "know" means "know me in themselves". We do not commit ourselves totally and exclusively to the light that comes through holy men of God, however sound it be. We are under duty bound to listen to the voice of the Lord Himself, and to follow Him.

DECEMBER 22nd

Till we all attain unto the unity of the faith, and of the knowledge of the Son of God. Ephesians 4. 13.

To have constant close association with people whose interpretation of Scripture does not tally with ours is hard for the flesh, but good for the spirit. We may have right views, but God is giving us an opportunity to display a right attitude; we may believe aright, but He is testing us to see if we love aright. It is easy to have a mind well stored with sound scriptural teaching, yet a heart devoid of true love. Oh, for Christian tolerance! Oh, for largeness of heart! Alas! that many of God's children are so zealous for the light they have that they immediately label as outsiders, and treat as such, all whose interpretation of Scripture differs from theirs. God would have us walk in love towards all who hold views contrary to those so dear to us. Nothing so tests the spirituality of a teacher as opposition to his teaching.

DECEMBER 23rd

But we have this treasure in earthen vessels, that the exceeding greatness of the power may be of God and not from ourselves. 2 Corinthians 4. 7.

Here we have possibly the clearest statement there is of the nature of practical Christianity. Christianity is not the earthen vessel, nor is it the treasure. It is the treasure in the earthen vessel. It must ever be a cause for great gratitude to God that no merely human weakness need limit divine power.

Too readily we think of power as the absence of the earthen vessel. Yet our blessed Lord Himself was for our sakes "crucified through weakness". There is nothing wrong in feeling weak. We are not meant to suppress all human emotions until we end up frigid as ice. Indeed, those who achieve this state are a constant drain on others around them, who must somehow make good their deficiency in natural affection if relationships are to remain even reasonably comfortable. No, we must rather allow God's Spirit to make His own use of our emotions. Of course He must be in command. Of course we must have the divine treasure—yes, but not in cold storage!

DECEMBER 24th

What, should I set this before an hundred men? 2 Kings 4. 43.

Faith is a most important factor in God's service, for without it there can be no truly spiritual work. But our faith requires training and strengthening, and material needs are a means God uses towards that end. It is not difficult to profess to have faith in God for a vast variety of intangible things. We may even deceive ourselves in this, simply because there is nothing concrete to demonstrate how lacking in faith we really are. But when it comes to financial needs, to food and drink and hard cash, the matter is so practical that the reality of our faith is at once put to the test. If we cannot trust God to supply the temporal needs of the work, what is the good of talking about its spiritual needs? We proclaim to others that God is the living God. Let us prove His livingness in the very practical realm of material things. Nothing will so establish in us the confidence in Him we shall certainly need to know when those other, spiritual demands come.

DECEMBER 25th

They fell down and worshipped him; and opening their treasures they offered unto him gifts, gold and frankincense and myrrh. Matthew 2. 11.

Matthew's is the Gospel of the King. "We are come to worship him," they said, and thereby at the outset established what was His right. For worship is everything. The more we worship, the more reason will God give us to do so. Before we pray let us worship; in preaching let us worship; in everything lift up adoring hearts to Him. This is the Church's work on earth today, to establish God's worship. Unless we give it to Him, God will have no worship here in this world. Of course we must not neglect other service, but let us always give to worship the first place. The wise men opened to Him their treasures. How can we hold back anything? And what we offer must be incense, not perfume:

incense that has to be wholly consumed on the altar of incense before its fragrance is released. That is true worship, and ours is the day when the Father seeks true worshippers.

DECEMBER 26th

When the fulness of the time came, God sent forth his Son, born of a woman. Galatians 4. 4.

When Jesus was born, Israel was a subject nation. The greatness of the kingdom was but a memory and the people of God paid tribute to Caesar. These were the days of Augustus, and Rome ruled the world. Yet in spite of appearances, He was born in the fulness of time. Everything was prepared. The Gospel of Christ was for all men; it could not be confined to one tiny nation. So God permitted Rome to absorb the world, and Jesus Christ was crucified in the Roman empire upon a Roman cross.

Rome's communications were good. Her roads and her ships went everywhere. Jews could come to Jerusalem at Pentecost, hear the Gospel, and carry it back home without crossing hostile national boundaries. Because Rome ruled, the apostles might travel freely from city to city within the Empire, speaking to men of the Saviour. The book of the Acts demonstrates the neutrality and the fairness of the secular authorities. Rome is likened in Scripture to a wild beast, but God who shuts lions' mouths had tamed her for His instrument. He shuts and no man opens; He opens and no man can shut.

DECEMBER 27th

There was a rainbow round about the throne. Revelation 4. 3.

The visions of Revelation chapters 4 to 11 are all related to the throne of God (4. 2); those of chapters 12 to 22 to the temple of God (11. 19). At the outset of the former ection we see a rainbow about the throne; at the outset of the latter we see the ark of the covenant in His temple. God's throne is established for the government of the universe. The full rainbow completely encircling it is His testimony to the universe that in all His administrative dealings, He that sits there will ever remain true to His covenant with mankind. God's temple is established as a habitation for Himself. The presence in it of the ark of His covenant, long since lost to unfaithful Israel as the centre of her national life, is God's testimony to Himself. It guarantees that nevertheless, true to His nature, what He has pledged Himself to do concerning His covenant people He will certainly perform. He cannot deny Himself. In Christ His faithfulness is assured—and we are in Him.

DECEMBER 28th

For this child I prayed; and the Lord hath given me my petition which I asked of him: therefore I also have granted him to the Lord. 1 Samuel 1. 27 f.

Do you notice two phrases here? To me they are exceedingly precious. Read them together: "The Lord hath given me ... I also have granted him to the Lord." In her distress she had besought the Lord for a son, and her request had been granted. What answer to prayer surpasses this one? The sum total of her request was for this child. Yet now, when she had received all she craved, she gave all back to the Giver. And as Samuel passed out of her hands, we are told, "They worshipped the Lord there."

When the day comes for me, as it came for Hannah, that my Samuel, in whom all my hopes are centred, passes out of my hands into God's, then I shall know what it really means to worship Him. For worship follows in the wake of the Cross, where God is All and in all. When our hands are emptied of all we hold dear and the focus shifts from ourselves to God, that is worship.

DECEMBER 29th

O my dove, that art in the clefts of the rock, in the covert of the steep place, let me see thy countenance, let me hear thy voice; for sweet is thy voice and thy countenance is comely.
Song of Songs 2. 14.

How hard we often find it to drag ourselves into His presence! We shrink from the solitude, and even when we do detach ourselves physically from things outside, our thoughts still keep wandering back to them. Many of us can enjoy working among other people, but how many of us can draw near to God in the Most Holy Place? To come into His presence and kneel before Him for an hour demands all the strength we possess. We have to be violent with ourselves to do it. But every one who serves the Lord knows the preciousness of such times, the sweetness of waking at midnight and spending an hour with Him, or waking early in the morning and getting up for an hour of prayer. Let me be very frank with you. You cannot serve God from a distance. Only by learning to draw near to Him can you know what it really is to serve Him.

DECEMBER 30th

I will most gladly spend and be spent. 2 Corinthians 12. 15.

In 1929, after prolonged labours in the Gospel, I returned worn out to my home town of Foochow. One day I was walking along the street with a stick, very weak and in broken health, and I met one of my old college professors. He took me into a teashop, where we sat down. He looked me over, and then he said, "Now look here: during your college days we thought a great deal of you. We had hopes that you would achieve something great. *Do you mean to tell me that this is what you are?*" On hearing this very pointed question, I must confess my first desire was to break down and weep. My career, my health, everything had gone, and here was my old professor asking: "Are you still where you were, with no success, no progress, nothing to show?" But the very next moment I really knew what it was to have the Spirit of glory resting upon me. The thought of being able to pour out my life for my Lord literally flooded my soul with glory. I could look up silently and say, "Lord, I praise Thee! This is the best thing possible; it is the right course that I have chosen!"

DECEMBER 31st

David, after he had in his own generation served the counsel of God, fell on sleep, and was laid unto his fathers.
Acts 13. 36.

David served in one generation, his own. He could not serve in two! Where today we seek to perpetuate our work by setting up an organization or society or system, the Old Testament saints served their own day and passed on. This is an important principle of life. Wheat is sown, grows, ears, is reaped, and then the whole plant, even to the root, is ploughed out. God's work is spiritual to the point of having no earthly roots, no smell of earth on it at all. Men pass on, but the Lord remains. Everything to do with the Church must be up-to-date and living, meeting the present—one could even say the passing needs of the hour. Never must it become fixed, earth-bound, static. God Himself takes away His workers, but He gives others. Our work suffers, but His never does. Nothing touches Him. He is still God.

INDEX TO SCRIPTURES

Matthew (*contd.*):

5. 44	Oct. 30
6. 5	Sept. 15
6. 6	Mar. 25
6. 9	Nov. 13
6. 10	Oct. 12
10. 29	July 18
11. 25	Sept. 26
11. 29	Nov. 15
11. 29	Nov. 16
14. 16	Apr. 11
15. 28	Sept. 1
16. 16	July 14
16. 17	Sept. 5
16. 19	Mar. 12
17. 27	Mar. 26
18. 18	Feb. 13
18. 20	June 15
19. 5	May 9
19. 8	Aug. 31
20. 6	Nov. 26
23. 8	Mar. 13
25. 6	Sept. 7
26. 10	Feb. 14
26. 39	Oct. 26

Mark:

6. 41	Jan. 1
6. 56	June 5
7. 29	Sept. 2
11. 24	May 28
12. 44	Oct. 8
14. 4	May 18
14. 9	Mar. 5
14. 72	May 30

Luke:

1. 38	Mar. 16
5. 5	Nov. 20
6. 19	Sept. 22
6. 38	July 12
7. 23	Dec. 8
7. 34	Oct. 9
9. 13	June 12
10. 33	July 2
10. 41	Jan. 23
15. 22	Feb. 19
17. 10	Dec. 20
17. 32	Oct. 2
18. 7	Oct. 13

John:

1. 17	Feb. 9
1. 36	Dec. 7
4. 23	June 16
5. 39	Aug. 29
6. 9	July 6
6. 10	Nov. 14
6. 11	July 5
6. 38	May 11
8. 32	Apr. 7
11. 26	Oct. 24
12. 3	Mar. 27
12. 28	Aug. 2
13. 14	Dec. 9
13. 17	May 4
14. 19	Mar. 10
14. 27	Feb. 7
15. 2	June 3
15. 4	Sept. 6
15. 5	Dec. 3
16. 13	Feb. 24
17. 3	June 17
17. 19	Apr. 8
17. 21	Oct. 29
18. 6	Feb. 6
19. 30	Jan. 26
20. 31	Aug. 5
21. 6	Dec. 5

Acts:

1. 14	Nov. 10
2. 1	Aug. 10
2. 21	Jan. 16
2. 33	Mar. 29
2. 38	Jan. 17
3. 6	Dec. 18
4. 7	Oct. 14
7. 55	Aug. 21
8. 29	June 26
9. 17	June 21
10. 44	Aug. 14
12. 14	Feb. 25
13. 2	June 11
13. 36	Dec. 31
14. 1	Sept. 19
19. 20	June 24
26. 19	Jan. 19
27. 23	Mar. 17

Romans:

5. 5	Aug. 12
5. 8	Sept. 28